RUINED A

Figure 1 "Coventry Cathedral ruined. November 14th, 1940"

Figure 2 "Coventry Cathedral rebuilt. An early conception of the new cathedral by the architect, Basil Spence"

Figure 3 Altar of Rubble, Charred Cross and Cross of Nails.

Ruined and Rebuilt

The Story of Coventry Cathedral 1939-1962

BY Richard. T. Howard
Provost of Coventry, 1933-1958

*"The latter glory of this house shall be greater
than the former, saith the Lord of hosts: and in
this place will I give peace."*
HAGGAI

Published by
Coventry Lord Mayor's Committee
for Peace and Reconciliation

on behalf of

COVENTRY CATHEDRAL

Ruined and Rebuilt
The Story of Coventry Cathedral 1939-1962
by Richard T. Howard

Publication History
First edition published May 1962 by
The Council of Coventry Cathedral
Second edition June 1962
3rd edition published November 2019 by
Coventry Lord Mayor's Committee for Peace and Reconciliation
https://coventrycityofpeace.uk/store/

ISBN
Ebook	9781871281538
Paperback	9781871281545
Hardback	9781871281552

FOREWORD

by John Witcombe
Dean* of Coventry

The night of Thursday November 14th 1940 marked a turning point in the history of Coventry, and especially of her Cathedral. The City of Coventry burned to the horror not just of those who lived here, but the wider nation.

The morning of Friday 15th marked a new beginning, as my inspirational predecessor, Provost Dick Howard, committed to rebuild the Cathedral 'to the Glory of God', and to an associated ministry of reconciliation.

Six weeks later, the BBC world service opened its Empire Broadcast on Christmas Day from the Cathedral Ruins. The service included these extraordinary words, "we are trying, hard as it may be, to banish all thoughts of revenge ... to make a kinder, simpler - a more Christ-Child-like sort of world in the days beyond this strife."

This book is an account of rebuilding not just a Cathedral, but rebuilding a relationship with the people of Germany. Many places have trodden this journey, but the story of Coventry, embodied as it is in its incredible building, has a unique symbolic strength that does transform lives.

Coventry Cathedral now leads an international network of over 200 centres for peace and reconciliation in the Community of the Cross of Nails. Reading this book was an important part of inspiring and equipping me for my own work.

---

* The official title for the leader of a cathedral was changed from Provost to Dean in the year 2000.

I am delighted that Coventry Lord Mayor's Committee for Peace and Reconciliation is republishing this work for a new audience, and I am grateful to the Chair, Philip Brown, for his work. I hope that it will find its way into the hands of those who will continue, each in their own way, the extraordinary work of Provost Dick Howard, recorded so powerfully here.

John Witcombe

November 2019

ORIGINAL FOREWORD

by the Bishop of Coventry,
the Rt. Rev. Cuthbert Bardsley, D.D.

Nobody is better qualified to write a brief account of Coventry Cathedral from the years 1939 to 1962 than the former Provost, the Very Reverend R. T. Howard. It was in the middle of his reign as Provost of the Cathedral that the destruction of that great building took place. With courage and prophetic foresight he recognized that it would be rebuilt and that the subsequent building would be even more glorious than the former. The bold, brief dictum went like a rallying cry across the world. At the worst moment of the war this assertion gave fresh hope and stimulus to very many people, both in Britain and German-occupied countries.

The City and Cathedral of Coventry became the symbol not only of man's determination to bring good out of evil, but it also became the symbol of the power of God to overrule disaster. Today, Coventry is a symbol of reconciliation and hope to very many people. That this is so, is due in no small measure to Provost Howard, who has written this brief and illuminating account of the Cathedral's progress during the past twenty-three years.

I hope that it will be widely read and that it will induce many who have never been to Coventry to visit the City and to see the majestic grandeur of the old ruins and the noble new Cathedral risen alongside.

CUTHBERT COVENTRY

1st January, 1962

ACKNOWLEDGEMENTS

The gratitude of the Cathedral Council and of myself is accorded to Mr George Rainbird of Rainbird, McLean Ltd for freely giving us the benefit of his invaluable advice and help in all matters connected with the publication of this book. His reader, Mr Charles Wrong, improved my first full version of Part I of the story by skilfully reducing it to the more readable length of this book. The original longer typescript has been bound in leather by Mr Rainbird for the Cathedral records.

I am personally grateful to Mr Harvey Warren of The Garden City Press Ltd for laying his wide experience of printing and publishing at my disposal. Archdeacon Proctor has rendered me a great service by reading the proofs and offering useful suggestions.

Acknowledgement is made for the use of photographs or blocks: Daily Mirror (fig. 1); P. W. Thompson (figs. 3, 7, 12, 13, 15, 22); Edwards The Printers (figs. 3, 4, 12, 16); E. W. Appleby (fig. 4); C. Birkett (fig. 5); Leamington Spa Courier (fig. 6); British Publishing Co. (figs. 5, 6); Birmingham Post (fig. 9) ; New York Times (fig. 11) ; Coventry Standard (fig. 19) ; A. Cooper (figs. 18, 23, 25); Associated Press Ltd (figs. 20, 26);Coventry Evening Telegraph (fig. 34); A. Cracknell (fig. 24).

Kenyon (fig. 28 (2)); Barret's Photo Press (28 (3), 31 (1)); Elliott Fry (29 (1), (2), (3)); T. F. Holte (30 (2)); Ambassador Publishing Co. (31 (2)); Ida Kar (31 (3)); Fayer (33 (1)). John Laing Construction Limited (fig. 27).

PREFACE

This book tells the story of how Coventry Cathedral was destroyed in the German air raid on the night of November 14th-15th, 1940. It tells how the Cathedral carried on as a place of worship and pilgrimage during the twenty years that followed. It describes how the building of the new Cathedral was planned; how the architects and designers were chosen; with what materials they worked, and what their designs mean. It flows on into the period when the new Cathedral undercroft became the Chapel of the Cross. It closes with the sight of the new Cathedral finished and ready for Consecration.

As Provost of Coventry from 1933 to 1958 I was naturally at the centre of this story. From 1958 to the time of approaching Consecration I have been in close and constant touch with the Cathedral as a deeply interested observer. I feel it is my duty to set down in writing what I have seen, in Part I of things in my own time as Provost, in Part II of things during the time of my successor. I firmly believe, as I hope to show, that working through all these events there has been a Divine Providence of Good, which it is a privilege to record.

I have had in view three classes of reader. There are the people of the City and Diocese of Coventry, who will be glad to have the story of their Cathedral set down for themselves and their children. There are the thousands of visitors, from all over the world, who have heard the fame of the Cathedral and come to see it for themselves. And finally there are the generations to come, for whom we pray that the Cathedral may stand unharmed for centuries, the sign of their faith as of ours.

The inscription on the title page of this book appears on a stone tablet placed on the west wall of the ruins[*] during the war.

The former glory of the old St Michael's was infinitely dear to those who knew it, but it has gone for ever from human sight. The latter glory has already come into view, and will capture the hearts and souls of our children and their children.

R. T. HOWARD

---

[*] The tablet is attached to the tower.

CONTENTS

TABLE OF FIGURES

PART I. 1939-1958

CHAPTER ONE

—

The Parish Church Cathedral of St Michael, Coventry

THERE have in the past been two Coventry Cathedrals, and now a third has come into being.

Our story of Coventry Cathedral begins with the Resurrection of Jesus Christ from the dead on the first Easter Day. The reason for the existence of every Christian church is that it may stand as a public witness to the fact of the Resurrection, and be a place where the worship of the Risen Christ is continually carried on.

The Gospel was brought to England in wave after wave during the first thousand years after Christ. In the seventh century St Chad came from the north to be the great missionary to the pagan Midlands. It is fitting that he is to be commemorated by having his figure inscribed among the British saints on the great glass screen of the new Cathedral. As a fruit of these Christian labours a nunnery was founded at the small town of Coventry. The most famous name connected with it is that of its abbess, St Osburga. She, too, will be commemorated on the glass screen, as will the great St Hilda, the abbess of Whitby in the north.

By the middle of the eleventh century Coventry had become an important town. Here was the castle of Leofric, Earl of Mercia, one of the three earls of the land under King Edward the Confessor. He and his famous wife, the pious and compassionate Lady Godiva, founded a Benedictine monastery in the town, and in 1053 built for it a large minster church. In about 1100 this church became the first Coventry Cathedral, sharing with Lichfield Cathedral the honour of being one of the two cathedral churches of the joint diocese of Coventry and Lichfield, under one bishop*, who lived at Coventry.

In the middle of the sixteenth century King Henry VIII dissolved the monastery and dismantled the cathedral. Coventry ceased to be a cathedral city for nearly four hundred years.

Meanwhile another great church had come into being in Coventry (figure 4). It was built between 1373 and 1433 as the Parish Church of St Michael, and was one of the largest and most beautiful parish churches in the country. It was built in the typically English Perpendicular style, at the very beginning of that period, when English architects and builders knew how to retain all the height and graciousness of the earlier Decorated style, and at the same time to impart to their churches an altogether new degree of slenderness, spaciousness and light. The ruins that still remain bear witness to the unsurpassed dignity and beauty of the building before it was destroyed. The unharmed tower and spire continue to testify to the miracles of architecture achieved by our fathers.

With the abandonment of the old minster Cathedral Coventry naturally became less important in the diocese than Lichfield, so that in 1700 the title of the diocese was changed from "Coventry and Lichfield" to "Lichfield and Coventry". Soon after 1800 the Coventry section of the joint diocese was detached from Lichfield, and made an archdeaconry of the diocese of Worcester.

During the nineteenth and early twentieth centuries the populations of Birmingham and Coventry increased enormously. First Birmingham hived off from Worcester as a separate diocese with a cathedral of its own.

---

* Robert de Limesey or Lymesey became Bishop of Coventry in 1102.

Figure 4 The Cathedral Church of St. Michael, Coventry. Built c. 1373-1433.

Then in 1918 the whole of Warwickshire, except Birmingham, was formed into a new diocese. The size and beauty of St Michael's Church, Coventry, as well as its location at the centre of the largest town, naturally singled it out as the obvious cathedral church for the revived diocese of Coventry. It was accordingly raised to the status of a parish church cathedral, becoming the second Coventry Cathedral.

The parish church cathedral is a new departure in English church organization. It remains the parish church of its own parish, but it also takes over all the functions of the Cathedral Church of the diocese. The vicar or rector of the parish church becomes the dean of the Cathedral, with the title of "provost".

The second cathedral had just time enough to grow to maturity before disaster overtook it. As a parish church it continued to perform those functions which any parish church, but particularly the central parish church of a great industrial city, seeks to fulfil towards the community. At the same time it sought with a considerable degree of success to establish itself in the affections of the parishes of the diocese as their mother church. Great diocesan services were held year by year in the Cathedral, which by reason of its open spaces was peculiarly suitable for such occasions. A high standard of musical worship was achieved under the leadership of three remarkable organists and choirmasters, Mr Hoyle, Dr Rhodes (afterwards organist of Winchester Cathedral), and Mr Alan Stephenson.

St Michael's was very fortunate in its founders, who had designed it as a parish church of such majesty that it was fit to rank as a cathedral. An association of Friends of the Cathedral was formed, with the purpose of caring for the Cathedral as a building, and preserving and beautifying its fabric for future generations. By 1939 plans for its enlargement and embellishment were already under consideration.

CHAPTER TWO

—

Coventry Cathedral in the First Year of the War

Those who remember the outbreak of the Second World War on September 3rd, 1939, will recall how tense the whole country was in the expectation of danger, and yet how the first few months of the war drifted by with almost no indication that the enemy was condescending to notice us.

Meanwhile the period was one of considerable discomfort, of which the most noticeable feature was the black-out. We groped our way along the pavements, our only guide being a small patch of light on the ground from an electric torch. We bumped into lamp-posts, or got totally lost. We drove our cars by means of a feeble side-light focused on the kerb. Yet there was one delightful compensation—even in the middle of the city we could see the night sky lit with stars. One moonlit night I climbed the Cathedral tower and looked down upon the city below. It lay dimly spread out in every direction, all harsh lines softened in the darkness. It seemed as though the Coventry of all the ages was peacefully dreaming of its past and future.

Day by day Christian people of all denominations met in the Cathedral to pray for the allied nations and their leaders, for the men and women in the Services, for the wounded and the bereaved, and for the enemy. The idea of a Chapel of Unity, which was later to take further shape, occurred to my mind for the first time during one of these services of intercession. The service was being finely conducted in one of the Cathedral chapels by the leading Baptist minister of Coventry, and I thought how good it would be if one such chapel could be made, for all time, a common place of prayer for all denominations.

One of the chief glories of our Cathedral was its spacious windows, covering vast areas of the walls. But they made black-out impossible. On Sundays in the winter Evensong had to be transferred to 3 p.m., not a time when the general public are disposed to come to church. So we devised a series of standard lamps with huge shades, and started a "People's Service" in the evening—something which we had long wanted to do, but had hesitated to begin in the face of old-established custom.

Then, suddenly, the pattern of the war changed. Denmark, Norway, Belgium, Holland fell. France was overrun. By June, 1940, Britain was alone in the world.

It was clear to all that the force that had struck down our friends would now be turned on us. In my sermons in the Cathedral I did what I could to hearten and encourage the people. I remember preaching on the text "He that endureth to the end shall be saved", and saying that if every church in the land were destroyed, it would be worth the sacrifice. This was, indeed, the general spirit. I have always believed that it was a spirit inspired in us by God Himself.

Already the sirens were wailing over Coventry. We were constantly being driven into the air-raid shelters, rather depressing places with rather depressing smells. It is extraordinary how cheerful we all were. On Sundays, and sometimes on weekdays, the clergy and ministers of Coventry would conduct late evening services in the shelters, and these were very popular.

The threat to the Cathedral was obvious, and, though we did what we could to meet it, the problem of protection was extremely difficult.

The roof, as you looked up from the interior and saw it above you, was a flat ceiling of oak, beautifully panelled, resting on huge beams which spanned the nave (figure 5). In about 1890 these beams were strengthened by thick steel girders, the existence of which the next generation seemed to have entirely forgotten.

Figure 5 Coventry Cathedral. The interior, 1935, before the destruction.

Above this inner ceiling, separated from it only by a space of some eighteen inches, and supported by cross-beams, was an outer wooden roof, with a covering of lead. This roof was nearly flat, sloping gently down from the central spine and it was easy to walk all over it. Likewise, the roofs of the aisles at the lower levels on either side were nearly flat.

Everything was strong and watertight, and—as far as all ordinary risks were concerned—fireproof. But we were soon to discover that such a roof was a terrible trap for incendiary bombs.

We took what steps we could to defend our Cathedral. It was suggested that the word KIRCHE, German for CHURCH, should be painted in enormous letters on the roof, so that the Germans might spare it. But we doubted whether they would respect such an appeal. It was suggested that the roof should be covered with a layer of earth a foot deep, to stifle incendiary bombs as they fell. But this was rejected as dangerous to the fabric, though I have sometimes wished that it had been attempted.

We decided that the beautiful fifteenth-century stained glass in the apse and the nave clerestories should be taken out and stored. This cost six hundred pounds and took several months, but finally all but a few fragments were safely stored in the cellars of Hampton Lucy rectory in the depth of the country. Here it remained undisturbed throughout the war, and in 1956 it was brought back to the undercroft of the new Cathedral.

A good supply of fire-fighting equipment—buckets of sand and water, stirrup pumps, shovels—was placed at key points on the ground and on the roofs.

A "Cathedral Guard" was established, consisting of four fire-fighters, to guard the Cathedral every night. It proved astonishingly difficult to keep this roster filled. Most of the able-bodied men of Coventry were either in the Services or employed at night in defending the many war factories of the city. On several nights shortly before the great raid my wife and I were alone on watch. Eventually we employed Mr "Jock" Forbes to be on duty every night from dusk to dawn. He was an elderly skilled stonemason, familiar with every inch of the Cathedral.

Some minor raids in August were followed by a lull; but then, in the middle of October, came a series of seven intense raids, each lasting for several hours. More than once incendiaries came very near the Cathedral; and from the roof we could see huge fires burning in the city.

On the night of October 14th an incendiary bomb pierced the lead roof and burst into flames on the oak ceiling below, where it could not be reached by stirrup pump or sand. Before the fire engines could reach the roof and extinguish the fire a thousand pounds' worth of damage had been done. Crowbars, axes and ladders were purchased as a further help against the recurrence of such a deadly danger.

Plans to remove the statue of St Michael and all precious woodwork to a place under the tower were on the point of being carried out.

With our new precautions we hoped that we should be ready for any emergency. But no one in Coventry—indeed, no one in England—was quite ready for what was to come.

CHAPTER THREE

—

The Destruction, November 14th, 1940

("The Story of the Destruction," written by the Provost a few days after the great raid, abridged.)

On the night of November 14th the Cathedral roof was slippery and shone white under our feet, for there was frost, and the bright light of the full moon was reflected on the lead.

The guard for that night consisted of Mr Forbes, aged sixty-five, myself, fifty-six, and two young men in their early twenties. Shortly after we had assembled at seven o'clock, the sirens sounded; and in little more than five minutes we heard the raiders overhead.

Soon the bombs started, and the horizon was ringed with a huge semicircle of light, showing that scores of incendiaries had fallen. More and more were showered down, nearer and nearer the Cathedral. Within a minute of igniting they exploded with a loud report.

Then, towards eight o'clock, the first incendiaries struck the Cathedral. One fell on the roof of the chancel towards the east end; another fell right through to the floor between the pews at the head of the nave, near the lectern; another struck the roof of the south aisle, above the organ. By shouting from the battlements to the police station the alarm for calling the fire brigade was given immediately.

The bomb on the chancel was smothered with sand and thrown over the battlements. The bomb on the pews was large, and took two full buckets of sand before it could be shovelled into a container.

The bomb above the organ had done what we most feared—it had fallen through the lead, and was blazing on the oak ceiling below. It took a long time to deal with. The lead was hacked open and sand poured through the hole, but the fire had spread out of reach. We stirrup-pumped many buckets of water before the fire ceased blazing.

Another shower of incendiaries now fell, penetrating the roofs of the Cappers' Chapel on the south side, and of the Smith's Chapel on the north side. These were ultimately subdued.

By this time we had been working for a long time at extreme pressure, and we were all very tired. Then another shower of incendiaries fell, four of them appearing to strike the roof of the Girdlers' or Children's Chapel above its east end. From below, a fire was seen blazing in the ceiling. Above on the roof smoke was pouring from three holes, and a fire was blazing through. These were tackled by all four of us at once, but, with the failing of our supplies of sand, water and physical strength, we were unable to make an impression; the fire gained ground, and finally we had to give in.

All this time we had been hoping every minute for the arrival of the fire brigade; yet we could hardly be surprised that none came, for the whole city was on fire. We learned afterwards that every engine was in use on some big fire, that many engines were trapped in narrow streets with a bomb crater at each end, and that engines coming in from other centres found the roads into the city blocked.

Looking inside the north door, we could see the roof burning fast above the Children's Chapel. One of the guard bravely attempted to get more water from the tap in the corner of the Smith's Chapel, which was our only source in the Cathedral. Smoke already filled this corner; he was nearly overcome and was helped away by another. We set to work to save such treasures as we could. We got out the altar cross and candlesticks and the standard candlesticks from the Smith's Chapel, and left them at the north door to be rescued next morning. It was a great grief that it was by now impossible to rescue from the Children's Chapel the beautiful wooden cross, with a carved figure of a child kneeling before it.

Next we went to the sanctuary and vestries to rescue the valuable ornaments and vessels there: the cross and candlesticks from the high altar, being the memorial to Provost Morton made by Omar Ramsden; a silver paten and chalice; a silver wafer box and snuffer; and a wooden crucifix. These were taken across to the police station.

Then we all went together to the south porch to rest under cover while waiting for the fire brigade. We wrapped ourselves in blankets from our camp beds, for we were streaming with perspiration, though the night was cold. We found it more frightening to be waiting there inactive with high-explosives falling near than to be active in the open.

At last, at about 9.30 p.m. the Solihull Fire Brigade arrived at the vestry door. Length after length of hose was fitted around the Cathedral with the help of the guard and of a bare-headed sixteen-year-old boy who seemed ready for any work and any risk. The hose was hauled up the ladder outside the north door to the roof, and at last a jet of water played upon the fire, which was raging over a large area of the roof on that side and among the pews below.

But, before it could do much good, the water ceased to come. Another series of hose lengths was run out to the hydrant by the corner of Priory Row and Priory Street, but still no water came. Later we learned that the water main had been shattered.

At the failure of the water we realized with intense consternation and horror that nothing could now save the roofs of the Cathedral nor any of the interior woodwork, which was already on fire over a wide area. We did not realize at this stage, however, that the pillars and interior walls were doomed.

Two of the guards now went to the crypt air-raid shelter to look after the people there. The other two, of whom I was one, began dragging as much of the sanctuary furniture as possible through the sanctuary doors into the vestries. Three altar frontals were removed from the case in the Mercers' Chapel and taken to the police station. Finally, we saw the two colours of the 7th Battalion, The Royal Warwickshire Regiment, hanging on the walls of the sanctuary, where they had been deposited for safe-keeping at a great service at the beginning of the war. I wrenched these down and placed them in the vestry.

Again and again I looked through the door from the boys' vestry into the sanctuary. I could watch the whole progress of the fire. It was pitiful beyond words to see the destruction of the ancient oak screen and carved misericords of the Lady Chapel, which would have been in safety if only the raid had come a few days later. It was even more distressing to see the flames consuming the memorial screen to Sir William Wyley's only son, killed in the last war. We were thankful that Sir William, who had died three months ago, had not had to bear the sight.

At about 10.30 p.m. the water came on again from another hydrant, and a hose was brought up the spiral staircase to the vestries and carried through the sanctuary door. For a while the water was played upon the Lady Chapel, but the pressure was low and it soon gave out.

The firemen now left the Cathedral for the last time. Nothing more could be done. They had worked with characteristic courage throughout their disappointing task. The risks they took for a building not their own were a constant stimulus to those Coventry people who were trying to save their own Cathedral.

I remained in the vestry long enough to carry out the Warwickshire colours, the altar service books, and the books of the Epistles and Gospels, to safety in the police station. These were the last things taken from the Cathedral.

It was now eleven. From then until 1.30 a.m. I was in the porch of the police station in St Mary's Street, along with a dozen of the Solihull Auxiliary Fire Service men. Here we could watch the gradual and terrible destruction of the Cathedral. High explosives were falling continually, some very near; but in the porch we were comparatively sheltered. I had the companionship of the firemen, who, like all watchers of the scene, were filled with horror.

At one point I clearly saw the pillar by the bishop's throne, and noticed that it seemed to have shrunk at the bottom in the intense heat of the burning screen. As far as I could make out, the falling of the pillars of the main nave arcade and clerestory walls was not due to high explosive, but to the falling of the roofs, and the consequent dissolution of the stresses on the slender and now weakened pillars, by which the heavy masonry above was supported. The steel girders, which had been encased within the principal beams across the nave, were twisted with the terrific heat, and must undoubtedly have helped to bring the walls down.

The whole interior was a seething mass of flame and piled-up blazing beams and timbers, interpenetrated and surmounted with dense bronze-coloured smoke. Through this could be seen the concentrated blaze caused by the burning of the organ, famous for its long history back to the time when Handel played on it.

About midnight the people sheltering in the larger crypt were alarmed by the roar of falling masonry above. Thereupon the two members of the guard in the crypt air-raid shelter removed the people to shelter elsewhere. From this time onwards the crypts were empty. They were completely unaffected by the fire, and remained intact and unshaken.

Not so the vestries, for which I had had such hopes. Burning masses of timber from the roof of the Mercers' Chapel filled the chapel itself and burst through the door into the vestry. The fire could be seen finding its way from vestry to vestry, till they were all ablaze. All the furniture and vestments left there were destroyed.

During the whole night the clock in the tower struck the hours, and, until the electricity supplies were cut off, the quarters also. There were many at a distance who took this as a sign that the Cathedral was intact. Even those who knew the worst felt the note of unconquerable strength sounding through that lurid night.

All night long the city burned, and her Cathedral burned with her—emblem of the eternal truth that, when men suffer, God suffers with them. Yet the tower still stood, with its spire soaring to the sky—emblem of God's overruling majesty and love.

By early morning the destruction was complete. Every roof was gone, and the whole Cathedral lay open to the sky. The matchless pillars, arcades, and clerestories * of the nave, chancel, and aisles were lying on the ground in long piles of broken masonry.

The encircling outer walls of all the chapels and the sanctuary stood in an unbroken line, completely enclosing the ruins. The walls of the five-sided apse were still standing with the traceries slightly damaged. The south porch, part of the older church which preceded St Michael's, was standing safely, probably owing to its groined roof.

The tower and spire were blackened on the side where the smoke had engulfed them, but otherwise they were as strong as ever.

"O ye fire and heat
bless ye the Lord:
Praise Him and magnify
Him for ever"

---

* Clerestories are high windows.

CHAPTER FOUR

—

Crucifixion Issuing in Resurrection

As I look back upon the stream of events that followed and still follow the destruction of the Cathedral, one tremendous fact stands out clearer than any other, and forms the central theme of this whole history.

On the night of its destruction, in an amazing and miraculous way, Coventry Cathedral became the living embodiment of the tremendous truth that, through the crucifixion and resurrection of Jesus Christ, all crucifixions in human experience can issue in resurrection. As I watched the Cathedral burning, it seemed to me as though I were watching the crucifixion of Jesus upon His Cross. After all, the Cathedral was not primarily a church belonging to man; it was the church of Jesus Christ. That such a glorious and beautiful building, which had been the place where Christian people had worshipped God for five hundred years, should now be destroyed in one night by the wickedness of man, was surely a monstrous evil that nothing could measure. It was in some mysterious way a participation in the infinite sacrifice of the crucifixion of Christ.

As I went with this thought in my mind into the ruined Cathedral on the morning after the destruction, there flashed into my mind the deep certainty that as the Cathedral had been crucified with Christ, so it would rise again with Him. How or when, we could not tell; nor did it matter. The Cathedral would rise again.

Through the ruined Cathedral we became aware as never before that God is Love, and that His Love is indestructible. However real and dreadful Evil may be, God is infinitely greater. He can make Good to triumph over Evil. He is ruling in Love to that End.

Over the years that have so far followed the destruction. Coventry Cathedral in God's mercy has proved the truth of this. There is not the slightest doubt that because of its destruction it has been the instrument of untold good to numberless people.

All that is now to be told of the first years after the destruction the transformation of the rubble into a place of worship, the building of an altar, the setting up of a charred cross, the fashioning of crosses of nails—sprang out of the Life that was working in and through the ruins. The rebuilding schemes that were planned and have gradually taken shape that have been the expression of the same inner urge. The new Cathedral is now finished; it stands beside the ruins of the old, and both together declare to the world this immortal truth—that in all human experience united with Jesus Christ, painful and sorrowful crucifixion will issue in joyful and glorious resurrection.

CHAPTER FIVE

—

The First Three Years After the Destruction, 1940 -1942

THE news of the blitz on Coventry was flashed round the world by radio next day. The Government considered it right to release the story of the all-night bombing of the civilian population, of the hundreds of lives lost, of the great damage to homes and factories, and of the destruction of the Cathedral. As the hours went on, and the courageous and cheerful spirit of the people of Coventry became known, "Coventry" sprang into fame as a world-wide symbol of the sacrifices which the peoples of the free world would have to endure before victory could be won, and of the spirit in which those sufferings would be endured.

It was natural that the destruction of the Cathedral should be the focus of this symbol. Soon the picture of the ruined building was in the newspapers all over the world. America was especially moved. The leading article of the New York Herald Tribune was typical of all:

> The gaunt ruins of St Michael's Cathedral, Coventry, stare from the photographs, the voiceless symbol of the insane, the unfathomable barbarity which has been released upon western civilization... No means of defense which the United States can place in British hands should be withheld.

Another American paper carried a cartoon of an arm rising out of the ruins with closed fist and thumb thrust up:

> The spirit of Coventry following the city's ordeal by air.

The most realistic and significant symbol of all appeared in the Daily Mirror (figure 1). It is a photograph taken immediately after the destruction from a window in the tower, clearly showing two steel girders lying in the form of a cross at the centre of the smoking ruins. *

The Bishop and Provost received hundreds of letters of sympathy, from every part of the world.

In Germany the people were informed that Coventry had virtually been wiped out by the Luftwaffe. The word "Coventrate" now signified the ruthless destruction which awaited all the cities of Britain.

Figure 6 The ruins after the destruction on November 14th, 1940, showing the iron girders, which had been encased in the beams of the roof.

My wife and I saw the Cathedral at 6 o'clock the next morning (figure 6). The ruins were still smoking. I was surprised to see that the Cathedral, now without pillars or roof, seemed to be far larger than before. The appearance of the ruins was so completely different from the Cathedral

---

* There is a tradition that it was the stonemason, Jock Forbes, who first noticed this cross, and pointed it out to the photographer.

before the destruction that it was impossible to think of them as the same building. But the long heaped-up piles of rubble seemed to retain an immense degree of beauty, as though they possessed something living and imperishable within themselves. This feeling has not diminished, but rather increased over the years.

From the length and intensity of the bombing we feared that thousands must have perished. But soon we heard, to our great relief that the number was not more than six hundred, about one in every two hundred of those in the city that night. This was dreadful enough, and tragic for the families who were bereaved. I remember wondering whether the life of a baby would be worth the saving of a Cathedral, and being quite sure that, valuable beyond words as was the Cathedral, one human life was yet more precious.

After the war we learned that, in proportion to the population, more people lost their lives from air raids in Coventry than in any other city in Britain. The toll of deaths on the night of the great November raid was chiefly responsible for this.

Back at home we found the Bishop of Coventry waiting to sympathize with us in our joint loss. The next to come was the Rev. Ingli James, the Minister of the Queen's Road Baptist Church.

At ten o'clock we returned to the Cathedral, and there I met the reporter of the Coventry Standard, Mr Edgar Letts, later its editor. Pointing to the ruins, I said, "We shall build it again." This was sent across the world, and among other things had the happy result of informing our relations overseas that I was still alive.

During the day, and for many days after, we gradually met the members of the Cathedral congregation, and other citizens of every walk of life. The theme of our conversation was always the same—thankfulness at seeing each other alive and unhurt, condolence at the loss of friends, homes, property, and places of business; but above all infinite grief at the destruction of our Cathedral.

The Visit of King George VI

"A report of the destruction reached King George in the afternoon" (of November 15th) "and he at once decided to visit the place on the following day in an effort to cheer the grievously afflicted citizens." Such is the record in the life of King George VI published in 1958. (Sir John Wheeler-Bennett, King George VI: His Life and Reign, p. 477.)

The King's arrival on the second morning after the raid took me completely by surprise. To the sound of cheering he entered the south-west door. I went forward to be presented to him, and he shook hands with me. I stood with him watching the ruins. His whole attitude was one of intense sympathy and grief. I told him how grateful the citizens of Coventry would be for this visit, and how it would encourage them.

The effect of the King's visit was indeed very great. We suddenly felt that if the King was there everything must be all right, and that the rest of England was behind us.

The King wrote in his diary: "I feel that this kind of visit does do good at such a moment, and it is one of my main jobs in life to help others when I can be useful to them." (Op. cit., p. 479.) Commenting upon all the King's visits to stricken cities, his biographer writes: "Here, in grim and starkly practical form, was pragmatic proof of his own theory of monarchy—a Sovereign standing at the head of his people sharing their dangers, deeply concerned for their suffering encouraging them in their continual determination to resist the enemy" (op. cit., p. 466).

On the spot where the King stood we set up a pillar made of pieces of carved stone from the rubble, surmounted with a stone inscribed "G.R. 16th Nov. 1940". Later the pillar was replaced by a tall pinnacle fallen from the walls, and on the base were inscribed the words:

King George VI stood here, 16th, November 1940, viewing the ruins.

This was called "The King's Pinnacle", and was an object of interest to King George on his two later visits to the Cathedral.

Figure 7 The Wyley Crypt Chapel (c. 1300) under the ruins, where the Holy Communion was celebrated on Sundays and Holy Days from 1940 to 1958.

Meanwhile, our first problem was how to carry on the worship of God on the site where He had been worshipped for nine hundred years. The small underground Wyley Crypt Chapel (figure 7), restored in 1932, had escaped unhurt, though all its approaches were damaged. We made it ready for use, only to learn that there was an unexploded bomb in St Michael's Avenue, opposite the entrance, and the public could not be allowed in. On the first Sunday after the blitz we were obliged to celebrate Holy Communion in the drawing room of the Provost's house.

On the second Sunday we established our Cathedral worship in the Wyley Crypt Chapel, with an 8 o'clock celebration of Holy Communion. This continued in an unbroken succession for eighteen years, until the last Sunday of 1958, after which it was established in the undercroft of the new Cathedral. At first the chapel was far from watertight. For many Sundays the rain dripped in from the ground above, now open to the sky. Two inches of sawdust was placed all over the floor to absorb the rain water. But gradually the roof was waterproofed, with a concrete pavement on the floor of the ruins, and a reasonable degree of comfort was attained. In spite of these difficulties we were very glad to be able to worship in this chapel, which in tiny form enshrined the beauty and majesty of our great Cathedral.

But this chapel, of course, was far too small for a full congregation, and there was no available hall nearby. We were most grateful to the Vicar of Holy Trinity Church, the Rev., afterwards Canon, G. W. Clitheroe, who invited the Cathedral congregation to worship with his own for Morning and Evening Prayer, and me to share with him in the conduct of services and in the preaching. This arrangement continued until the end of 1945.

On Christmas Day, 1940, Coventry Cathedral was selected to open the Empire Broadcast. The remnant of the Cathedral choir, a few boys who had not been evacuated or who were home on holiday, and a few men, stood with me under the tower and sang three verses of the Coventry Carol. Before the singing I gave a message to the Empire, ending with these words:

> Early this Christmas morning, here under these ruins, in the lovely little stone chapel built six hundred years ago we began the day with our Christmas Communion, worshipping the Christ, believe me, as joyfully as ever before. What we want to

tell the world is this: that with Christ born again in our hearts today, we are trying, hard as it may be, to banish all thoughts of revenge; we are bracing ourselves to finish the tremendous, job of saving the world from tyranny and cruelty; we are going to try to make a kinder, simpler—a more Christ-Child-like sort of world in the days beyond this strife.

We are in brave spirits, and can wish the Empire a courageous Christmas.

The broadcast was heard in all parts of the world, and we received messages from widely scattered listeners, thanking us for its heartening effect.

In January, 1941, I got Jock Forbes, the stonemason, to build an altar of stones from the rubble on the site of the high altar, and to set up behind it a cross made of charred beams found among the ruins. This work Mr Forbes* carried out with his characteristic skill and artistry. The coursing of the stones of the altar is faultlessly beautiful and dignified. The altar "board" is made from slate tombstones damaged in the raid. The cross, twelve feet high, stands in a tub of sand; the arms are bound by blackened wire (Frontispiece).

The effect of this Altar of Rubble and Charred Cross upon the minds and hearts of all who have seen them cannot possibly be estimated. The "Word of the Cross" was preached from now on in rubble and blackened wood. The Cross of Nails and the words "Father forgive" were added later.† Even without them the effect was often great, as you can read in this letter received from a lady in 1958:

I saw that burnt Cathedral with the Cross burnt but still standing. There for the first time I realized there was something true about the Bible. I had been to Sunday School as a child, but until that moment it really did not seem to mean much to me. I was lonely, away from home, and suddenly I looked up at this

---

* He continued as the Cathedral stonemason till 1947. He died in 1957.

† See Chapter thirteen.

Cross and I got on my knees. I got up, and I sincerely feel that Jesus came into my life in the Cathedral. From that day to this I have been a happy Christian woman. I am now happily married with three lovely sons, 9 years, 7 years and 3 years, who all go to Sunday School.

From the rest of the scanty remains of woodwork which escaped total destruction Mr Charles Ivens made many thousands of little crosses, the sale of which raised nearly two hundred pounds for the Cathedral Rebuilding Fund.

We were raided again in April 1941 on the night of Tuesday in Holy Week and very early on the morning of Good Friday. The bombs dropped this time had much more explosive power than those of 1940, and did almost as much damage to life and property as the great air raid. Two well-known members of the Cathedral congregation were instantaneously killed on Good Friday while visiting an old lady. They were Miss Ethel Loveitt, the Lady Worker at St Michael's Mission, who for nearly fifteen years had given herself devotedly to the service of the people of the mission district; and her sister, Miss Janet Loveitt, a lover of the Cathedral and famous for good works. That morning six incendiaries exploded along the open way up to the sanctuary and another in the sanctuary itself. Yet another dropped at the base of the Charred Cross behind the altar, but did not explode.

On Good Friday evening an open air service was held in the Cathedral ruins. A small Salvation Army band led the singing of the hymns. Owing to the destruction of the *Midland* (now *Coventry*) *Evening Telegraph* printing works in Tuesday's raid, this service could not be advertised, and the attendance was small; but its influence was great, since news of it went all over Britain and America. The theme of the service was: "It does not matter when you die; it only matters *how* you die."

On Easter Sunday we used the high altar in the ruins for the celebration of Holy Communion. The morning was warm and fine. The sanctuary was prepared with many flowers, especially daffodils. A pedestal of carved stones was set up for a credence table. The Bishop celebrated, assisted by me, and there were about forty communicants. The Cathedral was wonderfully beautiful in the soft clear light soon after sunrise, and all bore witness to a peculiarly ethereal sense of beauty that brought a message of Easter resurrection.

Such Communions were held every Easter—and are still held—except when the weather was bad, and also on Whit Sunday or Midsummer Sunday. Thus the Cathedral ruins were annually hallowed with the Eucharistic Offering and Communion.

The Coventry Cross of Nails

When the Cathedral was destroyed by fire, besides the rubble nothing was left but a few charred beams, twisted girders, bits of wire, and a great profusion of nails of all sizes lying everywhere, with every particle of wood burnt away from them.

On the morning after the destruction of the Cathedral, the Rev. A. P. Wales, the Vicar of a Coventry church which had suffered grievous damage, picked up from the Cathedral ruins three large sharp nails, and, binding them with wire into a cross, took it to show to the Bishop. That was the first cross to be made from Cathedral nails.

Three months later I took a young friend of mine, Stephen Verney, a student at Balliol College, Oxford, round the Cathedral. I noticed that he had picked up two small nails and bound them with a bit of wire into a cross. He said: "I have never felt the meaning of the Cross so powerfully as here in these ruins." In 1958 he became a Chaplain of the Cathedral.

Not long after this Mr Wales gave me a large cross of nails, now welded and chromium plated. Its shape was remarkable—the upright and the side arms being each half the length of the stem. Its symbolism of three nails was poignantly suggestive of the Crucifixion, its shining surface betokened the joy of the Resurrection. Its impact on the mind and heart was startling and profound.

Figure 8 Provost Howard presents an original Cross of Nails to a visiting delegation in Coventry Cathedral 1941.

From that year onwards the now famous Coventry Cross of Nails went forth on its path of power. I found that the gift of such a cross was appreciated beyond words, and forged a vital link between the Cathedral and the recipient. As a rule I gave them only to those who represented Christian churches or any denomination, or to public persons representing nations or communities.

By now the Cross of Nails has been given to over a hundred recipients, in every continent and in many countries. Kings, Queens, and Princesses have graciously accepted them. Bishops have received them as a bond between our diocese and theirs; Prime Ministers as a link between their country and Britain. Deans and Provosts have placed them in their Cathedrals as a symbol of our unity in the worship of God. Missionaries have taken them to be placed in mission churches in the heart of pagan countries. Scores of clergy and ministers have taken them away with a moving sense of gratitude or this new spur to devotion to Our Lord and fellowship with his disciples. In a few cases they have been given to individuals as a recognition of outstanding service and sacrifice for the cause of Christ and His Church.

After a time the need was felt for a place of prayer on the ground level. The south porch, with its Early English doorway and, groined roof, was obviously the most suitable place for solitude and small services. We gave it the name of the Chapel of the Resurrection, as a symbol of our faith that the Cathedral would rise again. It also bears the name of the Friends' Chapel, since the cost of restoration was defrayed by the Friends of Coventry Cathedral. It was dedicated in June, 1942, by the bishop, Dr Mervyn Haigh. About the same time a stone tablet was placed on the west wall, where the statue of St Michael had stood as a memorial to the First World War. It bore the words from the prophet Haggai which are given on the title page of this book*.

Meanwhile, the city and Cathedral of Coventry continued to attract famous visitors.

Twelve Canadian journalists, representing the Canadian Press, paid a visit in September 1941. The late Bishop Renison, afterwards Bishop of Toronto, was one of them.

---

* The text, from Haggai Chapter 2 Verse 9, can also be found on the old Cathedral tower.

Figure 9 The visit of the Prime Minister, Mr. Winston Churchill, on September 26th, 1941. With him are the Mayor, Alderman Moseley, and the Provost, the Very Rev. R. T. Howard.

Figure 10 The visit of King George VI and Queen Elizabeth on February 25th, 1942. Standing by the King is the Bishop, Dr Mervyn Haigh.

Each of them received a Cross of Nails as a great treasure and Bishop Renison made a short speech describing Coventry as "the Sacrificial City"—words which have become part of our history.

The Prime Minister, Mr Winston Churchill, came in September 1941, and greatly touched us by his gentle sympathy, (figure 9). The King, this time accompanied by the Queen, revisited us in February 1942, showing the utmost graciousness and kindness throughout their visit (figure 10). The Duke of Kent and the Princess Royal, Lord Halifax, at that time British Ambassador to the United States, Mr Menzies, Premier of Australia, and Mr Fraser, Premier of New Zealand were among those who visited the Cathedral in those early years.

During 1942 we lost Bishop Mervyn Haigh,* who went to be Bishop of Winchester. He had been our bishop for eleven years, devoting his great administrative ability to the care and progress of the Cathedral. The saintliness and dignity of his bearing, his intellectual attainments, and his statesmanlike speeches had won him universal esteem, and during the war his personality had done a great deal to maintain public morale.

On November 15, 1942, the victory of Alamein was celebrated by the ringing of the Cathedral bells. At the beginning of the war the ringing of church bells had been forbidden—it was kept as a signal that the country had been invaded. Now that we were free at last to ring our bells to celebrate a victory, we felt for the first time that final victory was in sight. This is how my diary for that day records the sound of the bells:

> They sounded infinitely glorious; like liquid music streaming down from the sky! Triumphant, happy, strong and sweet, challenging—everything truly Christian.

---

* He died on May 20, 1962, five days before the Consecration of the new Cathedral.

CHAPTER SIX

—

First Plans for a New Cathedral, 1941-1946

FROM the start the problem of rebuilding bristled with difficulties.

Would it be better to leave the ruins as a kind of war memorial in the form of a Garden of Rest? Should we try to rebuild the Cathedral exactly as it was before the destruction? If not, should we rebuild it in the Gothic style, or in a modern style, or in a mixture of both? Was it proper to rebuild at all, when the War Damage Compensation money might be used to build new parish churches? Could not Holy Trinity Church, Coventry, or St Mary's Church, Warwick, be made into the Cathedral Church? In view of the need for houses and hospitals, would it be better to postpone rebuilding to some date in the indefinite future?

One suggestion was that I should go to America and appeal for funds for rebuilding. There is no doubt that such an appeal would have been generously answered. But Coventry was not the only victim of the blitz. Dr Fisher, then Bishop of London and Chairman of the Central War Damage Committee, told me that there was a plan for appealing to America after the war on behalf of all the Christian churches that had suffered, and appeals for individual churches were being discouraged. When the war did end, this appeal was not made, as there were other countries in greater need of help.

The Cathedral Council met in March 1941 and carefully examined every suggestion. It finally decided to rebuild the Cathedral "on or near its present site". A Rebuilding

Commission was then appointed, consisting of twelve members of the Council under my chairmanship, "to explore the problems connected with the site and design of the new Cathedral and the appointment of the architect."

I first consulted three leading citizens of Coventry on the question of whether the old Cathedral should be left as a ruin or rebuilt, and, if rebuilt, in what style. Mr Joseph Holt, Mayor of Coventry at the outbreak of the war, thought that the new Cathedral should be a replica of the old, with improvements. Mr Ernest Ford, the City Engineer, who eight years later became the Chairman of the Reconstruction Committee, considered that, while a replica was not essential, the new Cathedral should follow the lines and style of the old one very closely.

However, Mr Donald Gibson, the City Architect, argued in favour of a modern design. He reminded us that the old cathedral builders had never hesitated to make the fullest use of every architectural development, nor to use quite different styles in the same building. He agreed that the colour of the new Cathedral should harmonize with the tower and spire of the old one; but he maintained that the juxtaposition of Gothic and modern styles should give a pleasing effect.

The Central Council for the care of Churches sent a delegation to examine the Cathedral and offer advice. This delegation reported that it should be possible to rebuild the Cathedral on its old site, retaining the outer walls.

Early in 1942, at my suggestion and with the support of the Bishop, the Cathedral Council invited Sir Giles Gilbert Scott to design the new Cathedral. I had greatly admired the new Liverpool Cathedral, which is his most famous work. I could think of no one whose work would more fittingly act as a bridge between the Gothic and modern traditions.

Sir Giles submitted designs in 1944 and 1945 which were approved by the Cathedral Council. However, it was found in 1947 that these designs did not find favour with the Royal

Fine Art Commission. In view of this, Sir Giles thought it best to offer his resignation, more especially as he now knew that the actual work of building could not begin for a considerable number of years, and he felt that by that time he would be too old to take part. The Cathedral Council felt obliged to consent to the verdict of the Royal Fine Art Commission, and so, with great regret, Sir Giles' resignation was accepted.

Before resuming the story of the planning of the new Cathedral, it is necessary to break off in order to describe the scheme for a Chapel of Unity and Christian Service Centre, which came to birth at this point.

CHAPTER SEVEN

—

The Chapel of Unity and Christian Service Centre, 1944-1946

A MOST welcome feature of the inter-war years in Coventry was the growing cordiality of the relationship between the Church of England and the Free Churches. There had been much co-operation in social service, many great united services in the Cathedral, several important joint pronouncements on the practical application of the Christian faith. In particular there had been close friendship between the leading clergy and ministers of the city.

Figure 11 The enthronement in the ruins of Dr. Neville Gorton as Bishop of Coventry, February 20th, 1943.

On February 20, 1943, Dr Neville Gorton was enthroned as Bishop of Coventry in the ruins of the Cathedral (figure 11). During the thirteen years of his episcopate his influence upon the reconstruction was very great. I was profoundly thankful to find that he shared my conviction that the Cathedral should be closely related to the civic community, and that it should give visible expression to Christian unity by incorporating a chapel for all Christian denominations. With his brilliant creative imagination the bishop seized on these ideas and fashioned them into a scheme for a Christian Service Centre and Chapel of Unity.

The Rev. Leslie Cooke, minister of the central Congregational Church of Warwick Road, Coventry, took a leading and constructive part in consultations with the Bishop and myself about the details of this scheme as it affected the Free Churches. The Free Church Federal Council of Coventry were fully consulted, and gave their whole-hearted consent. The scheme was published in 1944. It was proposed:

(1) To rebuild the Cathedral as the central church of the diocese. It would naturally belong to the Church of England, which would have the sole control of its services.

(2) To build, as an essential part of the Cathedral scheme, a Christian Centre of service to the community.

(3) To set up an endowment fund to staff both Cathedral and Christian Centre.

(4) To invite the Free Churches to a full partnership in the Christian Centre, which would be jointly staffed.

(5) To build a special Chapel of Unity attached to the fabric of the Cathedral itself. This chapel, as a building and as a place of worship, would belong to the Free Churches and the Anglicans together.

The following is an extract from the Bishop's statement:

> Wave after wave of immigration over twenty years has almost overwhelmed the community sense of Coventry. War has brought into it a flood of strangers from the entire British

Isles. The returning fighting man will hardly know its people...
The problem of transition back to peace will be overwhelming
for this unformed community unless we can set up some centre
of leadership. It is the church's great chance.

Eighty per cent of Coventry are without membership of
Church or Chapel. They are uprooted even in the secular
community of which they form a part. Yet Coventry has shown
itself capable of great loyalty and common service. There is a
friendliness to the Church. There are fine men and women and
young people ready to follow a lead. If they could see the
Cathedral standing for a new Christian leadership in an attack
on all the problems we have to face together, they could be
brought into the circle of Christ's action in Coventry...

I find on all sides a readiness to ask for cooperation from the
Christian community, "But," people say, "you Christians must
get together on a united front... The Christian Church exists to
break down barriers. Let Christians find unity, and in that unity
bring us the faith and leadership to find our unity." That is the
challenge; this is our response.

At the Christian Centre we shall provide for a headquarters
staff of Anglican and Free Church men and women capable of
detachment to tackle all these problems, to provide leadership
and the linking up of workers, and to create a Christian public
opinion and action beyond the bounds of the parish. Our
scheme has been drawn up after consultation between Anglican
and Free Church leaders. It has already received the approval of
the Cathedral Council and of the Coventry Free Church Federal
Council, and each of these bodies has appointed representatives
to collaborate in framing a constitution for the Christian centre.

In a Christian social attack Anglican and Free Churches in
Coventry are already fully co-operative in will. Give that co-
operation an instrument. Who is going to say it is wrong? The
mass of the community will say it is entirely right.

In co-operative witness the Anglican Church has a duty to
lead. It is the mother church of the country, still recognized as
such by the Free Churches, who sprang from it...

At no point in this scheme do we go beyond our Anglican
orders. Final forms of church unity are beyond our decisions...

This scheme provides for co-operation. Within that co-operation the Anglican Church keeps its integrity.

The Bishop's pronouncement was accompanied by public statements from leading Free Churchmen at the local and national level, giving their fullest support to the scheme. Among those who spoke strongly on its behalf were the Rev. E. B. Stringer, President of the Coventry Free Church Federal Council; the Rev. L. E. Cooke, B.A., Minister of Warwick Road Congregational Church; the Rev. L. F. Church, B.A., Ph.D., President of the Methodist Conference; the Rev. S. M. Berry, M.A., D.D., Secretary of the Congregational Union of England and Wales; the Rev. M. E. Aubrey, C.H., General Secretary to the Baptist Union of Great Britain and Ireland; and the Rev. W. T. Elmslie., M.A., General Secretary of the Presbyterian Church of England.

The Archbishop of Canterbury, Dr William Temple, gave his unqualified approval:

> I am deeply interested in the proposed scheme for the rebuilding of Coventry Cathedral and the attachment to it of a Christian Centre of Service to the Community with a Chapel of Unity connecting the two.
>
> It is, of course, essential that the Cathedral should be a purely and definitely Anglican church. That it should thus have associated with it a visible sign of practical means of united action seems to me a most happy inspiration, and I trust that the scheme will receive wide and enthusiastic support.

The scheme was studied with great interest by Church newspapers, some of whom welcomed it, while others criticized. But the general press was warm in its praises and approval. The great longing for Christian unity seemed at last to have some hope of being satisfied. Reunion now appeared to be a matter not of talk but of deed.

It was to be expected that exaggerated ideas of what the scheme proposed should be circulated. Some people wrongly supposed that in the Chapel of Unity full intercommunion had been established. This was unfortunate, because it caused unnecessary alarm and reaction in the opposite direction.

There were criticisms from both extremes. Some Anglicans sincerely believed that such a building as the Chapel of Unity purported to be ought not to be an integral part of an Anglican Cathedral. There were Free Churchmen who as firmly believed that a chapel where full intercommunion had not been achieved was no true Chapel of Unity.

The Anglican and Free Church promoters of the scheme maintained that, while they were under no illusion that the Chapel of Unity had solved all the problems of intercommunion and reunion, yet it was a real step forward in the direction of Christian unity. It expressed the fact that in many matters the unity between the Church of England and the Free Churches, though incomplete, is already fundamental. It was a means of reaching forward to closer degrees of unity, and it was a prophecy of the time that must surely come when the Will of Our Lord for the unity of His Church shall be completely fulfilled.

In 1946 the House of Clergy of the Convocation of Canterbury passed a resolution asking the Archbishop of Canterbury to appoint a joint committee of bishops and clergy to examine the scheme. The House of Bishops declined to grant the request, pointing out that the proposed interdenominational centre did not raise any new theological or ecclesiastical issue, and so did not bear upon the life of the Church in such a way as to make a joint committee desirable. Early next year the Archbishop invited a deputation of those members of the House of Clergy who were critical of the scheme to meet a deputation from Coventry Cathedral, including the Bishop, the Provost, the Archdeacon of Coventry and a prominent lay member of the Cathedral Council. The Coventry deputation gave a full account of the scheme, and were able so to satisfy the deputation of the Lower House that no further action was taken and all official criticism of the scheme in Convocation ceased.

In 1953, at the Church Assembly, a motion was proposed by a layman, criticizing Chapels of Unity as undesirable. After a vigorous debate, in which it fell to me, supported by the Bishop, to take a leading part, the motion was defeated.

During 1944 a constitution was worked out for the Christian Service Centre and Chapel of Unity. A joint committee of the Cathedral Council and the Coventry Free Church Federal Council was appointed for this task. Satisfying so many different points of view was not easy, but eventually a constitution emerged, and all the bodies concerned, the Synod of Clergy, the Cathedral Council, the Diocesan Conference and the Coventry Free Church Federal Council accepted it by overwhelming majorities.

The objects of the Christian Service Centre were defined as being to use the combined power of the Church of England and the Free Churches to strengthen their life and work among people in the county and diocese. It would seek:

(1) To deepen, widen, and intensify the corporate Christian life of the people in the Christian congregations;

(2) To encourage the Church in its work of evangelism;

(3) To relate every department of the life of the general community to the life of the Church;

(4) To strengthen the co-operation between Anglicans and Free Churchmen;

(5) To work towards the complete reunion of all Christian communions.

The governing body was the Joint Council, with twenty-four members; twelve being Anglicans, clerical and lay, representing the Cathedral and the Diocese, and including the Bishop and the Provost; and twelve being Free Churchmen, ministers and laymen; representing the chief denominations. The Bishop was the chairman. This Joint

Council had full administrative control over the Chapel of Unity and Christian Service Centre.

The first work of the Joint Council, early in 1945, was to accept from the Bishop and the Provost an offer of the large West Crypt under the Cathedral as a temporary Chapel of Unity, until such time as the new Cathedral and Chapel of Unity should be built. This fourteenth-century crypt, with its Gothic pillars and vaulting, was now transformed from a very dismal, damp, cold and dark chamber into a beautiful, well-ventilated, well-warmed and brightly-lit chapel, holding about a hundred people. It was equipped with furniture made by country craftsmen, and provided with an Oxford lectern bible, a Cross of Nails, and a remarkable oak plaque depicting the Risen Christ.

Figure 12 The temporary Chapel of Unity established in 1945 in the West Crypt (c. 1300) under the ruins.

On the fifth anniversary of the destruction an inaugural service was held in the ruins at night, and thousands attended from all over the diocese. The temporary Chapel of Unity was dedicated in the presence of clergy, ministers and laity of the diocese, the mayors and town clerks of the boroughs, and twelve representative Christian men of various denominations from various countries of the world. Led by the Bishop and the Mayor of Coventry, the congregation pledged themselves toj unity by saying these words aloud:

> I promise by God's help no longer to mistrust the grace of God in my fellow Christians;
> to show them Christlike love in word and deed;
> to spend myself for the perfect unity of all Christian people;
> to do all I can to make my church a better instrument of Christ's love for men.

In May 1946 an appeal was launched, with Colonel D. G. O. Ayerst as its able and imaginative organiser, for the purpose of building and endowing the Christian Service Centre and Chapel of Unity, and for providing an endowment for residentiary canons of the Cathedral. It had the good wishes of Dr Fisher, the Archbishop of Canterbury; of the Rev. Frank H. Ballard, M.A., the Moderator of the Free Church Federal Council; and also of such representative persons as the Dowager Lady Reading, Field Marshal Lord Montgomery, Sir Anthony Eden, and Sir Stafford Cripps. The literature of the appeal described in glowing terms "this new kind of Cathedral", "a kind of university of christian living at the elbow of everyone who needs its help", "the mother church of all its people in a truer sense than has been possible for three hundred years." Queen Mary presented a beautifully bound bible, which had been presented to her by the Y.W.C.A. on the occasion of her marriage. The King and Queen headed the list of donations with a gift of five hundred pounds.

The chief item of costs for which the appeal was made was the endowment of a considerable number of wardens, who would carry out the actual work of the Christian Service

Centre in the spheres of the home, education, industry, music, the arts, healing, and so on.

When the appeal had run for six months the sum of money collected amounted to eighty thousand pounds. Then the unfortunate thing happened. The architectural basis of the appeal was Sir Giles Scott's design, and this was now abandoned. The appeal collapsed with the design. It could not be renewed until a new design was produced, and that would not be possible for several years. The money subscribed was put by against the day when the new Cathedral, with a new design for a Christian Service Centre and Chapel of Unity should be ready.

Moreover, it was impossible to work the scheme without wardens, and not yet possible to provide for them. This meant that the Christian Service Centre had to be indefinitely postponed; and so far it has not been possible to resume work on it. It remains an essential part of the new Cathedral project, and of our hopes for the future.

The temporary Chapel of Unity in the Cathedral crypt, however, went on from strength to strength throughout the years. It is true that without the Centre it had no active body behind it feeding it with objects for prayer. Nevertheless, in the Providence of God, the Cathedral staff were able to make it a living and powerful force.

Its most constant use was as a place of pilgrimage for visitors. They came in tens of thousands from every continent. Whenever possible they were taken down in parties to the Chapel of Unity, and the nature of the chapel, as a place of worship belonging to all Christians, was explained to them. We believe that many of them were moved with an intense sense of the presence and love of God. They were invited to say aloud the prayer of all Christians, the Lord's Prayer, in their mother tongue. Some who had not prayed for, years now prayed again. They left the chapel with a new light burning in their souls, a new longing for unity, a new determination to see unity in their own church.

But there is more to be told. United services were frequently held in the chapel for different kinds of religious and civic groups: Rover Scouts, the Coventry Guild of Citizens, the United Nations Association, the Bible-Reading Fellowship. In the Week of Prayer for Christian Unity the chapel became the rendezvous for prayer for Christians from the churches of Coventry. Among the regular events were a service in German for Lutheran Christians in Coventry conducted by Pastor Kurtz; a monthly study group attended by Christians of several communions; and a service every term for secondary school girls. Courses of lectures on the Christian Faith were well supported.

It can confidently be said that for a growing number of Coventry people the temporary Chapel of Unity became the proper meeting-place for all Christians of goodwill. And so it remained for fifteen years until its work was done and it passed to other uses.

CHAPTER EIGHT

—

The Harlech Report and the Architectural Competition, 1947-1951

No time was lost by the Cathedral Council in recovering from the shock of having to abandon Sir Giles Gilbert Scott's design. In January 1947, at the same meeting as that at which his resignation was perforce accepted, the Council decided to appoint a commission of public men to advise on the problem.

The Chairman of the new commission was Lord Harlech. Its members were the Very Rev. H. A. Jones, Provost of Leicester Cathedral; Sir Philip Morris, Vice-Chancellor of Bristol University; The Right Rev. L. D. Hammond, Suffragan Bishop of Stafford; Sir Percy Thomas, Past President of the Royal Institute of British Architects; and the Rev. E. Benson Perkins, of the Methodist Church.

The work of the commission was immensely thorough, and occupied the first half of 1947. They made their own careful and independent examination of the site and the ruins and the problems connected with them. They invited the opinion of every imaginable group of persons who might have any interest in the new Cathedral; and they gave special weight to the views of the City and Church authorities.

Their report appeared on July 7th, 1947. It was a comprehensive survey of the problem, with plans and photographs; and its principal recommendations, which were unanimous, were as follows:

(1) The new Cathedral should be built as nearly as practical on the site of the last.

(2) The existing walls were not strong enough to be incorporated in a new building, having deteriorated in the previous six years.

(3) The Cathedral should be built of red sandstone, and in the Gothic tradition.

(4) It should be large enough to accommodate one thousand worshippers in the nave and aisles, and have room in the choir and choir aisles for two hundred clergy.

(5) The altar should be at the east end, and visible to as many of the congregation as possible.

(6) The architect should be selected by an open competition, organised by the Royal Institute of British Architects.

(7) Building operations should be controlled by a Building Committee of seven laymen, including one Free Church member.

In general the report was warmly welcomed. Coventry people did want their Cathedral back, and back on its former site. But the recommendation that the architect should be obliged to work in the Gothic style aroused a great deal of controversy. Some people, who had been afraid that a modern cathedral would clash with the surviving tower and spire, were grateful for the insistence on a Gothic building. But many others—and among them the whole architectural world, including the Royal Institute of British Architects, the Coventry City Architect (Mr Donald Gibson) and the Coventry Society of Architects—protested vehemently. They urged that in an open competition the architects should be left free to build in whatever style they thought best, and they gave the warning that some of the best present-day architects would refuse to compete unless they were allowed this freedom. This protest was supported by a leader in The Times.

The Diocesan Conference in its advisory capacity gave its "general approval" to the report. The Cathedral Council, which is the authoritative body, unanimously gave "general approval" to the report but with the important proviso that the architect was to be free to make his own choice of style, provided that the new Cathedral was built in harmony with the tower and spire.

The Building Committee, soon renamed the Reconstruction Committee, was constituted without delay. (The names of its members appear in Chapter nineteen.) Its first chairman was Colonel The Honourable Cyril Siddeley, afterwards Lord Kenilworth. Its secretary was Captain Norman T. Thurston, M.C., who had been the Chief Officer for Civil Defence in Coventry from 1941 to 1947. The choice of Captain Thurston was very fortunate. He had proved his exceptional ability in all fields of organization and personal relations. He was deeply interested in the Cathedral and all its schemes.

While the Reconstruction Committee was preparing for the architects' competition, Mr Donald Gibson, the City Architect, saw to the carrying out of another recommendation of the Harlech Report—the layout of the ruins.

First, the rubble was removed, and the whole interior was covered with a layer of ashes. Large areas were then covered with a further layer of earth, and turfed. The central aisle and side-walks were gravelled. Finally, flowers were planted, and the eight Hallowing Places* were built (Figure 13).

The transformation was miraculous and complete. The rubble had been beautiful, especially when covered with flowering willow-herb; but it was austere, desolate, and uncomfortable. Now the whole scene spoke of peace. The Altar of Rubble and Charred Cross in the sanctuary came fully into their own. From that time onwards the ruins have been more mysteriously powerful than ever in their religious appeal, and have made all visitors feel that the trouble they

---

* See Chapter thirteen.

have taken in making a pilgrimage has been abundantly worthwhile.

Figure 13 The ruins cleared of rubble and laid out with gravel aisles and paths and grass lawns, in 1947.

The shattered windows of the tower were filled with new glass; the wooden louvres of the windows in the spire above the octagon were repaired. This took some time, and required the skilled work of steeplejacks.

But the chief work of the Reconstruction Committee from 1947 to 1949 was the purchase of new land on the, north side of the Cathedral, between the graveyard and Priory Row. This sloping land lies roughly between Priory Street and Holy Trinity old churchyard, to a depth that carries it down to the wall of the old Triumph works. The land was owned by six different owners, all of whom, however, proved willing to sell. Negotiations for the purchase were successfully carried through by the Chairman and Secretary, and the required land passed into the possession of the Cathedral.

In the middle of 1949 Mr Ernest Ford, O.B.E., retired from being City Engineer, a post which he had held with great distinction for twenty-five years. He and I had been personal friends for fifteen years, and I had had every opportunity of assessing his ability. At my request he agreed to join the Committee, and Colonel the Hon. Cyril Siddeley most generously resigned from the chairmanship to allow Mr Ford to take his place.

And now we were ready for the architects' competition.

This was to be sponsored by the R.I.B.A., whose president at that time was Mr Waterhouse. He informed us that the R.I.B.A. was not in favour of making the competition an international one. There were twelve thousand architects in Great Britain and the Commonwealth to choose from. He promised that the panel of judges would be most carefully selected, in such a way that architects of all schools would feel confidence in their judgment; and that they would be men who understood the function of a Cathedral as a place of Christian worship.

In due course a panel of three assessors was chosen: Mr (afterwards Sir) Edward Maufe, R.A., LL.D., F.R.I.B.A., the architect of the new Guildford Cathedral; Mr (afterwards Sir) Howard Robertson, M.C., A.R.A., F.R.I.B.A., afterwards President of the R.I.B.A.; Sir Percy Thomas, O.B.E., LL.D., F.R.I.B.A., Past President of the R.I.B.A.

While all three assessors were worthy of the task, Mr Maufe was particularly competent to judge in the ecclesiastical field, Mr Robertson in the artistic field, and Sir Percy on practical matters.

Before drawing up the conditions of the competition the assessors visited the Cathedral, made their own scrutiny of the site, and had prolonged discussions with the Reconstruction Committee, in which every aspect of the situation was carefully examined.

The conditions finally laid down for the competition ran to fifty-six clauses, and there is no room to reproduce them here. This is an outline of the more important ones :

(1) Each competitor must submit his designs, anonymously, by July 2nd, 1951.

(2) The cost of the new Cathedral was given as £825,000. This was based upon the most careful estimate of the promises of the War Damage Commission, money already given or promised in response to former appeals and a margin of extra money which it was believed would readily be subscribed to a public appeal in the future.

(3) Competitors were given a plan of the site within which the Cathedral should be built. This included the site of the old Cathedral and the graveyard, and the new land purchased beyond Priory Row. It would not be essential to plan the Cathedral directed to the east.

(4) The tower should be retained, either separate or part of the new Cathedral.

(5) The walls of the ruins might be retained or removed at the discretion of the competitor.

(6) The altar should be placed towards the east, in such a position that as many as possible of the congregation should have a clear and uninterrupted view. There should therefore be no screen.

(7) The Cathedral should seat 1,200 amply spaced, with a maximum of 1,750 when filled to capacity with all space occupied by chairs.

(8) The pulpit and lectern must each be given a position of importance and dignity in relation to the altar and congregation.

(9) Provision should be made for eight "Hallowing Places" (see Chapter thirteen).

(10) A place should be found within the precincts for the Charred Cross, Cross of Nails, Altar of Rubble, and the stones bearing the words "Father forgive".

(11) The Chapel of Unity should be contiguous with the main Cathedral building, forming an integral part of the whole architectural grouping of the Cathedral.

(12) The Christian Service Centre should form an architectural composition with the Cathedral, but need not necessarily be attached to it.

(13) No restrictions were imposed in regard to style or materials; but it was pointed out that the existing tower, the nearby Holy Trinity Church, and the fourteenth/fifteenth-century St Mary's Hall, were built in stone, and that a similar good sandstone, light pink-grey in colour, was still available.

(14) No perspective drawings were allowed.

The book of conditions opened with a preface signed by the Bishop and Provost. Accompanying the book but not part of it were three longer memoranda by the Bishop, the Cathedral chapter and the Joint Council. These statements described their views as to the functions of the Cathedral and the Chapel of Unity, and were intended for the guidance and inspiration of the competitors as they planned their designs.

In response to an advertisement in the leading national newspapers, between five and six hundred competitors applied for the book of conditions. Many of them wrote to ask further questions, and in the end the answers to a hundred questions were made into a second book and sent to all the competitors.

In the end the number of architects competing was 219. Their anonymous drawings (which, if placed side by side, would have reached for nearly three-quarters of a mile) were privately exhibited in King Henry VIII School, Coventry, during the last week of July 1951.

The assessors arrived at the beginning of August. Before proceeding to judgment they joined in a special service of prayer in the Crypt Chapel—the culmination of six months of prayer in all the parish churches of the diocese.

CHAPTER NINE

—

The Winning Design and its Architect, 1951

ON August 15th, 1951, the report of the assessors was delivered in the great hall of King Henry VIII School to the Reconstruction Committee, who sat facing the screen upon which the large drawings of the still anonymous winning architect had been hung.

In their report, the assessors said:

> Although we consider the general level of the designs is disappointing, yet we are happy to report our conviction that the competition has succeeded in bringing forth several designs of great merit, and one of outstanding excellence.

> In selecting this design we not only feel that it is the best design submitted, but that it is one which shows that the author has qualities of spirit and imagination of the highest order. He lets the conditions grow under his hand to produce, a splendid Cathedral, and as the conditions are unusual, the resulting conception is unusual, revealing the author's ability to solve the problem of designing a Cathedral in terms of contemporary architecture.

The report continued with high praise for the various parts of the design.

The assessors then handed to the chairman of the Reconstruction Committee the sealed envelope containing the name of the architect. It can well be imagined with what intense interest the envelope was opened, to reveal the name of Mr Basil Spence, O.B.E., F.R.I.B.A., of 40 Moray Place, Edinburgh. One of the committee had met him quite casually a few months before, but otherwise his name was unknown to any of us.

Mr Spence was immediately informed by telephone of his success. The news was then released to the Press, and once more Coventry Cathedral became front-page news.

Mr Spence's own description of his design was contained in his report to the assessors, accompanying his drawings, and now preserved in the Cathedral archives. The following extracts will reveal the vision that was in his mind:

> THE IDEA. As the Cathedral stands now, it is an eloquent memorial to the courage of the people of Coventry. It is felt that the ruin should be preserved as a garden of rest ... and the new Cathedral should grow from the old and be incomplete without it.
>
> The altar is the heart of the new building ... it can be seen from the ruined nave. The five glass screens dividing the porch from the nave are of clear glass, and, on warm summer evenings, can be lowered, so that the Cathedral is open. There is no physical obstruction, on such occasions as these, between the whole population of Coventry and the altar. St Michael's Avenue, the traditional right of way, remains, except that it passes under the Cathedral porch within sight of the altar.
>
> As the Life of Our Lord commenced with a star, the first element of the Cathedral plan is the Chapel of Unity, star-shaped ...
>
> Much thought has been given to the position of the Chapel of Unity in the Cathedral plan. It must express Unity, and is the Chapel of the Holy Spirit ...
>
> The Chapel's shape represents Christian Unity; in elevation it is shaped like a Crusader's tent, as Christian Unity is a modern Crusade ...
>
> The author of this design does not see this building as a planning problem, but as the opportunity to create a Shrine to the Glory of God.

The features of the new design are now familiar in all their detail from the successive guides to the new Cathedral published from 1952, and from the Cathedral as it has actually been built. But there may well be readers of this history who have no access to a cathedral guide. Accordingly I shall summarize here the chief points of the design, as was originally put forward by Mr Spence. Later the reader will see the ways in which this design was modified.

The tower and spire of the old Cathedral were retained to fulfil the same function in the new one. The ruins, with the Sanctuary, Altar of Rubble, Charred Cross, and Cross of Nails, were preserved as a memorial "garden of rest" and as a forecourt and approach to the new Cathedral.

The new Cathedral was to be built out from the old Cathedral on lower ground to the north, and constructed in pink-grey sandstone throughout. Its great proportions would give an awe-inspiring sense of majesty (figures 14 and 15).

Figure 14 The new Coventry Cathedral. Photograph of a drawing by Sir Basil Spence in 1957.

A low porch, supported on slender columns, was designed to stretch over St Michael's Avenue and be the vestibule to the new Cathedral.

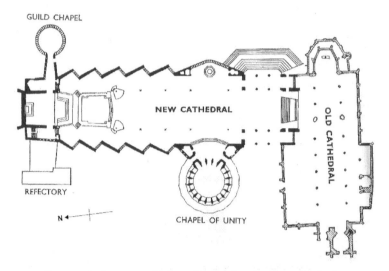

Figure 15 The ground plan of the old and new Cathedrals.

The west wall* would contain a very large glass screen, which could be automatically lowered into the ground. On this screen would be engraved the figures of saints and angels. Through the screen the whole interior would be visible from the ruins and the porch; thus the old and new Cathedrals would be linked together as one.

Within the Cathedral the altar would be visible from practically every part of the building.

On the east wall, behind the altar, there would be a great tapestry depicting the Crucifixion.

The font would be inside the door on the right, with a conical canopy reaching nearly to the roof, lit by a great baptistry window with 195 lights.

---

* The glass screen is physically at the south end of the new Cathedral, the altar is at the north. But since the eighth century, it has been common practice to use terms such as "east end", "west wall", "north aisle" as if the church were oriented with the altar at the east end, even in those many churches where the altar end is not actually to the east. It is sometimes called the "liturgical east".

On the left would be the Chapel of Unity, built in the shape of a crusader's tent. The ground plan would be shaped like a star, betokening "peace on earth, goodwill towards men". The fourteen windows would be filled with stained glass.

The walls of the Cathedral would be five bastions of stone on each side, set at an angle to give strength.

The windows of the nave would be in five pairs, also set at an angle, rising from the ground to roof level, throwing the light in waves up the Cathedral towards the altar. They would be filled with stained glass, in significant colours and figures symbolizing the pathway of human life from childhood through adolescence to middle age and old age, and on to the After Life.

In the recesses between the walls and the windows would be the Hallowing Places, with great sculptures on the wall-faces opposite the windows.

In the chancel would be the pulpit and lectern and the bishop's throne, placed prominently before the people. The organ would be high up on either side at the end of the aisles.

Over the whole nave and choir, stretching from end to end and reaching to the roof, would be the vault, supported by two rows of slender concrete columns on either side.

Behind the east wall would be the Lady Chapel, the Children's Chapel, and a new Chapel of the Resurrection.

At the south east corner of the new Cathedral would stand a Guild Chapel, circular in shape. At the north east corner would stand the Christian Service Centre, balancing the Guild Chapel.

Two days after the adjudication Mr Basil Spence came to Coventry and met us all. From that day there began an intimacy of friendship and mutual appreciation that has grown throughout the years.

In his early years as an architect Mr Spence was the admiring pupil of Sir Edward Lutyens when he designed the new Roman Catholic Cathedral at Liverpool. At the end of 1950, when the competition for Coventry Cathedral was announced, he was very busy building the Ships and Seas Pavilion for the South Bank Exhibition in the Festival of Britain. It had been his life-long ambition to design a Cathedral, and now, at forty-three, he decided to enter.

Visiting Coventry in the autumn, he had been tremendously moved by the sight of the ruins and the sanctuary, with its Altar of Rubble, Charred Cross, and Cross of Nails. Thereupon the vision had come to him of a new Cathedral, which would demonstrate the truth of the Resurrection as the ruins spoke the truth of the Crucifixion. He worked for months mainly at night, seeking to translate his vision into concrete form.

Here I should record my personal estimate of Basil Spence as an architect, a man, and a friend. It has been arrived at as a result of many years of close and constant contact with him. As an architect, I believe him to be an inspired creative genius. He has the extraordinary power of a genius to see a vision of what is absolutely beautiful and right, and to create the concrete form in which his vision can come true. Sometimes I have met his new ideas at first with startled opposition, but in the end I have always been convinced that his judgment was both beautiful and true. As a man he is profoundly religious, aware of God, steeped in prayer, devoted to God's glory, humble before the Source of his inspiration. As a friend he is affectionate and loyal, a charming and witty companion.

From the beginning the Reconstruction Committee were in favour of Mr Spence's design, and they grew steadily more enthusiastic. Among those who expressed great satisfaction were the Bishop, the Mayor of Coventry, and Mr Ford, the chairman of the Reconstruction Committee. The committee's enthusiasm was greatly increased when Mr Spence, after touring the cathedrals of the Continent, laid before us a number of very beautiful perspective drawings of the new Cathedral. During the months of September, October and November, 1951, Mr Spence's design went through all the necessary stages of acceptance, being passed by the Cathedral Council, the Joint Council, the City Planning and Redevelopment Committee, and the Royal Fine Arts Commission.

Not that the Cathedral as finally completed is exactly as Mr Spence first designed it. Throughout the work of rebuilding his creative imagination has been continually at work, and the original design has frequently been modified as the result of some new vision, often arising out of some difficulty or necessity.

Here are some of the changes since the original design:

The tapestry. Instead of the Crucifixion the subject for the tapestry is now the ascended Christ in the glory of God the Father. I suggested this to Mr Spence at our first meeting and he immediately agreed.

The porch had been much lower than the roof of the nave and he felt that it was an inadequate link between the old and the new. He therefore raised it to the height of the roof, giving it greater dignity. In this second stage there was to be a great triumphal arch of stone, taking the place of the five windows of the north wall of the ruins. Finally this gave way to a delicately poised roof gently reaching over the north wall. One window of the north wall has been moved to allow a way through from the ruins into the porch.

The east wall, against which the altar was to be placed, has been removed, and the wall of the Lady Chapel behind the altar has become the east wall of the Cathedral, against which the tapestry is hung. This gives a much more spacious vista at the east end over and beyond the altar, and saves the altar from being dominated by the tapestry.

Instead of making *the glass screen* movable downwards into the ground, Mr Spence decided to make practically the whole west wall an immovable screen or wall of glass. This has greatly increased the extent to which figures can be engraved on the screen.

The *transomes* (or horizontal stone bars) of the great nave windows, instead of being placed at equal lengths above each other, as in a ladder, are placed at alternating heights of short and long. This adds a sense of interest and liveliness as the eye moves upwards and downwards along the windows.

The vault was originally to consist of large curving surfaces in concrete. Now it is crystalline or prismatic in shape formed between the concrete structural ribs by an infilling of timber louvres, through which shafts of artificial light can pass to illuminate the nave.

The nave has only one row of slender columns on either side, instead of two.

A fleche, or tall slender spire, rises from the roof above the point where the line between the font and the Chapel of Unity crosses the nave.

The Chapel of Unity is joined to the Cathedral by a short cloister instead of a massive stone structure. Still star-shaped in the ground plan, and in elevation like a crusader's tent, it is composed of a circle of tall graceful buttresses supporting a low conical roof. It is built of concrete faced with green slate instead of pink-grey stone, and its shape makes a delightful contrast to the simpler nave wall.

The interior walls were originally designed to be faced with pink-grey stone like the exterior. They are now faced with concrete blocks, covered with sound-absorbing plaster coloured white. While saving a considerable sum in construction costs, this brings out to a maximum degree the colours of the pink sandstone mullions of the windows, the tapestry, the stained glass; and the furnishings and ornaments.

Finally, a word on the style of the new Cathedral.

The adoption of a "present-day" style is the expression of a faith that God has given to present-day men creative powers of their own and new tools of His revealing, and that, if men will use these powers and tools, courageously to build to His glory, He will honour their efforts with aesthetic success. This was the faith of English builders all down the centuries of creative building. Norman, Early English, Decorated, Perpendicular, Renaissance, Georgian—each in its day was the expression of such a faith, and each was successful and has lasted. Moreover, each in its turn was able to blend with what went before and what came after. We hope and believe that our faith will have the same success.

CHAPTER TEN

—

Storms Followed by Calm.
1951-1954

THE storm of controversy that broke over Mr Basil Spence's design for the new Cathedral was unparalleled in the history of architecture. It raged with fury, and spread across the world. Articles on the controversy appeared in the newspapers and magazines throughout the British Commonwealth, in America, and many other countries.

From the first it became clear that the design, described by one of the assessors as "a landmark in architecture" and by its architect as "a prayer in stone", was supported by the overwhelming weight of informed opinion. The architectural world welcomed the design as signalling a new age in Britain. Modern architecture would now create, to the glory of God, a building which by tradition is the greatest of all buildings—a cathedral.

On the other hand, many critics—even clergymen—resorted to extraordinarily violent language to express their dislike of the new design. The new Cathedral was called "a monstrosity", "a horror", "an aesthetic outrage", "pagan", "a super-cinema", "a mausoleum". There was a great deal of protest, though not all in such unrestrained language.

One thing that many people failed to realize was that the drawings published in the Press were those which had been presented to the assessors in the competition, for which perspective drawings had been prohibited. All drawings were in section or elevation, and purely technical in character. When drawn in colour and perspective, let alone actually built, the Cathedral would look completely different.

Eventually such drawings appeared, and much of the criticism was silenced.

But the trouble went deeper than this. The fact has to be faced that there are many people to whom modern art is repugnant; and when this art invades the realm of religious buildings, which ought in their opinion to be beyond criticism, their repugnance turns to violent anger. Older people, brought up from childhood to take traditional art for granted, are particularly prone to feel like this. Yet there are very many older people who, without losing their affection for traditional art, have been able quite happily to adjust themselves to modern ideas.

The Cathedral authorities did not let themselves be too worried by the controversy. They were almost unanimous in their conviction that Mr Spence's design was right for the Cathedral. Their case was argued vigorously in the Press. "Wait and see," they said in effect, "what the building will be like when it is built. We believe that you will then be convinced, as we are now, that our design is the right one."

A set of lantern slides of Mr Spence's drawings and paintings was produced. Every autumn and winter from 1954 onwards, Captain Thurston and I, together or separately, have taken these slides round, visiting half the parishes of the diocese, in village, town, or city, and scores of societies clubs, and schools. They have always had the desired effect. People have found their conception of their new Cathedral radically changed, and have been captivated by its beauty.

It is accordingly not surprising that over the years opinion has been steadily swinging round to favour Mr Spence's design. Frequently opposition has turned into warm support. No doubt there will always be some who prefer the traditional to the modern style, and there may always be a small minority who are repelled by modernity in any form. But for some years now, as far as the general design of the

Cathedral is concerned, the storm of controversy has given way to general calm.

For a time we had to face opposition on the City Council for an entirely different reason—the housing shortage.

This had already made itself felt before the Second World War owing to the influx of people into Coventry during the 1930's. The destruction of five thousand houses by air raids made things immeasurably worse. Although vast new housing estates had arisen, at the end of the war there were more than ten thousand families without houses of their own. Naturally, they looked with suspicion upon all proposals to rebuild the Cathedral. They feared it might hinder the provision of homes for themselves.

The Bishop and I were deeply sympathetic. We shared their feeling that houses must come before the Cathedral. When the first rebuilding plan of Sir Giles Gilbert Scott was published in 1944, the Bishop gave a public pledge that the re-housing of the population and the rebuilding of bombed hospitals, parish churches, and chapels, must have priority, and that the rebuilding of the Cathedral must in no way interfere with this.

But we knew that it would take some years before work on a new Cathedral could be started, and that during those years the housing problem would be gradually eased by the building of new housing estates. We therefore saw no reason why we should not go ahead with our plans. Unfortunately, the homeless thousands found it difficult to see things in that light. All they saw was that the Cathedral was making progress, if only on paper, and their houses were not.

When Mr Basil Spence's design was published in 1951, the building issue again leapt into prominence. By now, six years after the war, many new houses had been built; but thousands were needed. It was pointed out that the new Cathedral would be built of stone, and that the stonemasons and craftsmen required would be drawn from a totally different labour source from that required for house building. On the other hand, the new Cathedral would also need concrete, which was in short supply for all purposes, housing included.

The Reconstruction Committee, knowing that it would still be several years before the actual building could begin, went steadily ahead with the long preparations that had to be made.

In early 1954 the issue came to a head. We were now quite ready to start building. The City Council had always been warmly in favour of Mr Spence's design, and desired that at some future period the Cathedral should be built. But now they were busy on their great new building programme—shops, hotels, health centres, offices, baths and library for the new City Centre. They had Government building licences to spend half a million pounds annually on these projects. Meanwhile, there were thousands of houses yet to be built. Some leading members of the City Council firmly and sincerely believed that it would be better to finish off the city centre and the housing estates, and let the Cathedral wait for ten years.

In February 1954 they were able to carry the City Council in a resolution that the time was still inopportune for starting the Cathedral.

This was indeed a sudden earthquake—and the newspapers of the world recorded the shock. Those who still disliked the Cathedral design rejoiced that the City Council had intervened on Heaven's behalf! By this time the Reconstruction Committee had learned from Government sources that the situation with regard to concrete and other materials, and with regard to labour, had so far improved that the starting of the new Cathedral would in no way hinder the progress of either housing or the City Centre operations. We felt that if the City Council could spend half a million annually on such public buildings as shops, hotels, offices and public houses, we could reasonably ask to be allowed to spend a fifth of that amount on a Cathedral.

We wrote to the Press, stating our reasons for thinking that, although there were other churches in the city, a Cathedral such as had been designed was a unique necessity for the diocese. Furthermore, since the Cathedral reconstruction was a matter for the nation as a whole, we thought we had better submit the issue to the Government to decide. We therefore applied for a licence to spend £985,000, which would be spread over a number of years.

The Minister of Works, Sir David Eccles, invited a deputation from the City Council to put their case before him. Having considered both points of view, he wrote on April 23rd, 1954, to the Reconstruction Committee, saying that he had decided to issue the licence as soon as we were ready to start work. At the same time he wrote to the Lord Mayor of Coventry stating his reasons, and ending with the following memorable statement:

> My duty as Minister is to enquire whether the Cathedral could be built without interfering with any other work in progress or ready to start. I am satisfied that it could. It would be an abuse of my powers to refuse a licence because some people thought this particular building unnecessary.
>
> I hope, however, that the decision will be accepted on wider grounds. The Cathedral is not a building which concerns Coventry and Coventry alone. The echo of the bombs which destroyed your city was heard round the world. We cannot tell how many people are waiting in this country and abroad for this church to rise and prove that English traditions live again after the blitz. The threat of far worse destruction is with us demoralising and corrupting our thoughts. We have never had a greater need for acts of faith.
>
> The people of Coventry can be assured that the most careful thought has been given to all the arguments for and against the granting of a licence. Is it too much to hope that they will now welcome the end of controversy, and unite to aid the building of a great and beautiful church?

This letter was sent to the Press, and made a profound impression throughout the world. It is greatly to the credit of the City Council that they accepted the verdict of the Minister, and gave all the necessary facilities for beginning the work.

Throughout this brief storm the personal relations between the leaders of the City Council and the Church authorities had remained friendly. Throughout the long and often difficult years of negotiation, the Mayors and Lord Mayors* of Coventry have consistently shown helpful co-operation and unfailing goodwill to the Cathedral.

---

* The Mayors of Coventry were granted the title of Lord Mayor from the time of the Coronation in 1953.

CHAPTER ELEVEN

—

New Works of Art in Tapestry, Glass and Sculpture

A CATHEDRAL should be the centre of a vital connection between the arts and the Church. In the case of our ancient cathedrals the buildings themselves are mighty achievements in architectural art. In the case of our new Cathedral we believe that, by giving a talented modern architect the liberty to create freely in his own style, we shall not only have another triumph of architecture, but shall also give an important contribution and encouragement to Art as such.

The building of a new cathedral gives a wide opportunity to the crafts in glass, sculpture, woodwork, and, in our instance, tapestry. From the very beginning Mr Basil Spence asked that, wherever such works of art were required in his Cathedral, the very best artists in the country—or outside it if necessary—should be enlisted for the task. The Reconstruction Committee enthusiastically agreed. I shall now tell how these artists were appointed, and how our choice has been justified by their creative achievements.

The Tapestry

It was a brilliant and daring idea to cover the whole of the east wall with a tapestry. The traditional east window lets in the early morning sunlight, but it dazzles the eye, and takes to itself the glory which belongs to the altar and the celebrant. A tapestry reflects light without dazzle. It forms a beautiful and impressive background to the altar, without in a way competing with it.

On December 18th, 1951, Mr Spence recommended to the committee the artist he had chosen to design the tapestry: Mr Graham Sutherland. Mr Sutherland was already regarded as the most eminent and widely honoured of our younger painters. He was held in the highest estimation in Italy, France and the United States. The committee immediately approved Mr Spence's choice.

Mr Sutherland's task was an extremely complicated one. The tapestry would be the dominating feature of the Cathedral, and the congregation would have no choice but to see it all the time, by night as well as by day. The theme would have to present the timeless truths of the Christian Faith as based on Scripture, and do this in such a way as to be theologically sound.

The subject, chosen by myself with the agreement of the Bishop, would be Christ the Redeemer in the Glory of the Father, shedding His Spirit upon the Church. It would combine in one unity of composition the following four themes: the Glory of the Father (represented as "light unapproachable" around the figure of Christ); Christ as Redeemer, His hands and feet showing the marks of His Passion; the Holy Spirit, resting on the Apostles; and the Heavenly Sphere, with St Michael and other celestial beings.

Mr Sutherland realized that he was faced with an immensely difficult task. It would have been easier to depict Christ on earth, the Resurrection or Ascension, or even the Last Judgment. But Christ in the Glory of God is in the infinite sphere of eternity, yet to be depicted as human, and as One who has suffered. Mr Sutherland has told me that he regarded this as the most difficult task of his artistic life and considered that if he could succeed in it, it would be his greatest work.

Mr Sutherland and Mr Spence together studied the Book of Revelation in the Bible, as giving the original Christian description of the worship of Christ in Heaven. They chose the Four Living Creatures in the Bible called the "Four

Beasts"—the lion, the calf, the man, the eagle—as being the best representation of the community in Heaven worshipping God.

For six years Mr Sutherland grappled with his problem with the help of the constant prayers of the Cathedral. His first maquette was produced after two years. He invited the Bishop and several members of the committee to see it, and we were deeply impressed. A year later, in December 1954 and January 1955, he presented his almost completed maquette to the Reconstruction Committee, the Cathedral Chapter, and the Cathedral Council. But it needed another two years to bring his design to perfection, and he found it necessary to alter the whole colour scheme, and to change Our Lord's arms from being stretched outwards to being lifted up in the attitude of blessing. It was not until September 1957 that he brought his final maquette to Coventry, where it received the entire approval and warm gratitude of the three responsible Cathedral bodies (figure 16).

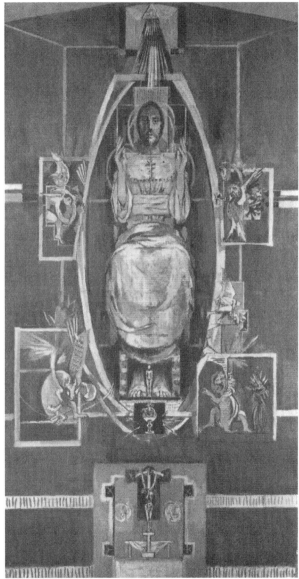

Figure 16 The tapestry which covers the east wall of the new Cathedral. Photograph of the design in colour by Graham Sutherland.

Soon after Mr Sutherland began the designing of the tapestry, it was decided to place it on the, east wall, forty feet behind the altar, which would now mask the lower part of the tapestry from the sight of the congregation in the nave. The lower part would therefore become the background of the Lady Chapel.

At first it was recommended that the subject of these lower panels should be scenes from the life of the Blessed Virgin Mary, as recorded in Holy Scripture. However, Mr Sutherland came to feel more and more strongly that, as the subject of the main tapestry was Christ in Glory, the Passion of Christ should be the prominent theme in the lower part. In the end he placed the Crucifixion by itself in the centre lower panel, leaving the side panels plain. This decision by the artist is right beyond all possibility of question, since it places Our Lord's death in the proper relationship to His Resurrection and Ascension. Those who attend the services of the Mothers' Union in the Lady Chapel will feel that they like the Mother of Our Lord, are standing by the Cross.

Mr Sutherland's design was issued to the Press of the world in March 1958. The controversy aroused was immediate and very sharp, perhaps sharper than at any previous stage of the rebuilding.

This was because the figure represented was that of Our Lord Himself. Many, to whom abstract representations of human qualities were unintelligible and repulsive, found it horrifying and blasphemous to see their Lord so different from traditional pictures of Him; and no words were strong enough to express their indignation. All we could do was to explain that to many the face and figure of Christ was the most beautiful they had ever seen; that it was not in any case supposed that His face in glory was like anything that could be depicted upon earth; that whatever was depicted could at best be only a representation of the fact of His ever-living Presence with us on earth; that the strange attitudes of the Four Living Creatures were powerful abstract symbols of the response of created beings to the discovery of their Creator—startled awe (the eagle), the offering of energy (the lion), humble diffidence (the calf), awestruck groping (the man); and that, when it is woven and hung and has had time to be thoroughly absorbed, it will increasingly stimulate and satisfy the imagination and the souls of men.

The Cathedral tapestry was to be the largest ever attempted, and would be seen in a more impressive setting and viewed by more people over the years to come, than any previous tapestry. Obviously, therefore, the choice of weavers was a problem of great importance. The tapestry-weaving industry on any large scale has practically died out in Britain. Where could we go for weavers?

Eventually, early in 1958, the work was entrusted to the firm of Pinton Frères, at Felletin near Aubusson in France. While some were disappointed that this great feature of the new Cathedral should not be made by British craftsmen, the fact was that only in France could the tapestry be made in one piece. More important still was the fact that this firm was generally believed to be the best in the world at this craft at the present time. The director of the firm and supervisor of all the work is Madame Marie Cuttoli, who began to revive the French tapestry industry in 1928, and is now regarded as one of the world's greatest authorities in this field.

The Ten Nave Windows

To anyone standing at the east end of the new Cathedral it appears as a vast lantern of coloured glass. The five windows on either side face the altar, and appear close together, almost as one window. They are seventy feet high with four lights across each window.

The choice of craftsmen to execute these ten windows constituted one of the greatest commissions to be given for ecclesiastical stained glass for very many years.

Mr Basil Spence wanted the ten windows to be designed as a unified whole, and to be executed together as a group by modern British designers. He wanted them to be conceived in the contemporary and semi-abstract style, so as to be in keeping with the architecture. His final choice for the work was the Royal College of Art, to whom the commission was given in October 1952.

The Royal College, the leading school in the country for artists and designers, had for many years maintained a Department of Stained Glass. Under the Principal, Mr Robin Darwin, this department had lately shown a vitality and a readiness for experiment that had put new life into this great but neglected art.

Mr Darwin entrusted the direction of the work to Mr Lawrence Lee, A.R.C.A., who was head of the department. Associated with Mr Lee were two outstanding artists in this field: Mr Geoffrey Clarke, A.R.C.A., and Mr Keith New, A.R.C.A. Mr New was working in America with the Corning Company and Steuben Glass, but we secured his release to work on the Cathedral.

Mr Spence's original plan was that the nave windows in pairs, going from west to east, should represent the progress of man through the ages of his life: childhood, adolescence, middle life, old age and the After Life. The three designers of the R.C.A., in collaboration with Mr Spence later elaborated this theme by making the windows on one side of the nave represent the divine aspect of man's life and those on the other side the human aspect.

It took them nine months to work out the coloured designs. In June 1953 they invited our inspection of these. We were greatly impressed with the depth and accuracy of their theological interpretation of the Christian Faith, with the vivid imaginativeness of their symbols, and with the brightness and beauty of their colours.

Three years later, at midsummer 1956, six of the ten windows were finished and were exhibited at the Victoria and Albert Museum in London. Even under artificial light their magnificent colours aroused universal admiration. The symbolic forms in the windows met the mixed reception with which the reader must now be familiar. Many people were quite unable to understand the symbolism, and expressed disappointment or irritation. Others who were equally puzzled were content to enjoy the beauty of the shapes without understanding exactly what they meant. Others took great pains, with the help of a written guide, to fathom the meaning of each window, and were richly rewarded for their trouble.

By the middle of 1958 the remaining four windows were ready. The whole set of ten windows were stored at the Royal College of Art, waiting for the time when the nave would be ready to receive them.

The Glass Screen

Answering the tapestry at the east end, the great glass screen or wall at the west end was a unique creation of the mind of Mr Basil Spence. Its function is to influence the mind of the worshipper as he enters the Cathedral from the porch.

The screen is seventy feet by forty feet, and through it you are able to see the whole of the Cathedral from the porch or ruins, and to look out on the ruins from inside.

From the first the architect's plan was to have the figures of saints (especially martyrs) and of angels engraved on the screen. Here again was the challenge of finding an artist who could design a very large number of figures to be engraved on clear glass. After long consideration Mr Spence's choice fell upon Mr John Hutton, who was warmly recommended by Sir Edward Maufe, one of the assessors. Mr Hutton was engraving some remarkable windows for the new Commonwealth Air Forces Memorial at Runnymede which Sir Edward was designing. A New Zealander, then forty-seven years old, he is a self-taught artist who has become one of the leading mural painters in the country and highly skilled at the art of glass engraving. When he visited

Coventry the Bishop and I were greatly impressed with his charm, insight and sensitivity.

We learned that there were to be four rows of saints on the screen: five on the topmost row, nine on the next two, and finally eight, alternating with rows off lying angels. In close consultation with Canon Moore Darling and Canon Proctor, I came to the conclusion that the best choice would be as follows:

> Top row: Five Old Testament figures—Abraham, Moses, David, Elijah, Isaiah.

> Second row: Nine New Testament saints—the Virgin Mary and the Christ Child in the centre; the four Evangelists Matthew, Mark, Luke and John on the left; John the Baptist, Peter, James and Paul on the right.

> Third and fourth rows: Seventeen British figures—the four patron saints, George, Patrick, Andrew and David; Alban Columba, Augustine, Aidan, Oswald, Cuthbert, Chad, Hilda, Bede, Margaret, Alfred, Osburga (abbess of the ancient convent at Coventry), à Becket.

> Across the bottom of the screen at ground level there are six panels for angels. For these we chose the most prominent of the angels of the New Testament: the angel of the Annunciation, the angel of the Garden of Gethsemane, one of the two angels of the Resurrection, one of the two angels of the Ascension, the angel of the Everlasting Gospel, and the angel of the measuring line of the City of God (from the Book of Revelation). At the suggestion of the Cathedral Chapter, St Michael the Archangel and Patron Saint of the Cathedral, is placed at the centre of the top row of angels.

The Bishop agreed with our choice, and it was approved by the Cathedral Chapter and Council in 1953.

For the symbols which traditionally always accompany the figures of saints an expert in the diocese on heraldry, Mr H. T. Kirby, of Gayden, Warwickshire, supplied a well informed and interesting list, which I communicated to Mr Hutton.

Armed with these particulars, Mr Hutton set out on his long task. Here in his own words is a description of his method of work.

> The design of each figure is first worked out on black paper with white chalk. The first drawing is a small scale one, the result of many sketches and studies.
>
> From this a full-size drawing is made, also on black paper with white chalk. Tracings are then made of the body of the figure which are transferred to the glass.
>
> Large grindstones are used to engrave the body in very low relief—not more than one eighth of an inch at the deepest point. The draperies, face, hands and feet are then engraved over this surface with small grindstones of various degrees of coarseness, using flexible drive equipment to obtain the greatest possible freedom of drawing. Parts of the engraved surfaces are brought to a high polish in order to give variety of reflection and therefore as much life and movement as possible to the whole design. In some lights these polished facets show up strongly in relief and in others they disappear almost completely.
>
> The main problem in such a large screen, almost entirely covered with figures, is to keep the idea alive and intense.
>
> The work, from the first rough designs to the finished glass panels will have taken about ten years.

The Baptistry Window

As you enter the new Cathedral, the first blaze of coloured light falls from the great baptistry window on the right. The slightly bow-shaped window is immensely broad, being fifty-six feet across, and reaches from ground level to the roof eighty-four feet above. It has 195 lights or apertures, each of them in a deep cavity of its own formed by the stone mullions, and each well separated from its neighbours. It is just possible to see all the lights if you stand directly in front of the window, but, as you move away, the lights soon narrow and disappear behind the mullions.

Fitting these 195 lights with stained glass in one harmonious pattern presented a problem of peculiar difficulty. It was four years before Mr Spence had decided on his artist.

The art of glass staining has been in transition for a considerable time. There has been a movement away from the purely traditional style, but there were only a few in Britain who had reached a settled competence in contemporary colour and design. It was tempting to look for an artist on the continent, where the modern style had reached a higher creative level.

Eventually his attention was attracted by new work in stained glass that was being undertaken by Mr John Piper. Like Mr Sutherland, Mr Piper was already one of the best known of modern English painters, and his standard of excellence was beyond all question, particularly in the realm of colour. Now he had begun, with great success, to design stained-glass windows. His co-worker in making the glass was a young artist craftsman, Mr Patrick Reyntiens. Together they were working on the glass for the memorial east window of Oundle School Chapel.

Mr Spence was convinced that here were the two artists he needed for the baptistry window. On his recommendation, Mr Piper was appointed by the Reconstruction Committee in 1955.

The subject of the window, naturally, is the glory of baptism as the new birth into the family of Christ. It had originally been proposed that each of the separate lights should contain pictures of the childhood of the saints; but Mr Piper eventually decided that a separate picture in each of the lights would give an uncomfortably "staccato" effect. A later project, of a symbolical picture in the form of a large pattern covering many lights, had to be given up, because the stonework separating the lights is too broad to make this possible.

In the end Mr Piper decided to make colour itself the instrument for imparting to the heart and mind the glories of baptism, without using figurative shapes or symbolic forms.

Being a master of colour, he was eminently qualified to use this method. In December 1957 he placed his completed design before the Cathedral Chapter, who were unanimous in their praise.

In presenting his design, Mr Piper described the window as in reality a pierced screen. He emphasized that his design had to be extremely simple, not only because of the great size of the window, but because it must be regarded as an introduction to the elaborate designs of the ten nave windows, and must not conflict with them. His design accordingly, was an abstraction in colour, and any interpretation of it would be open to the individual.

The Bronze Statue of St Michael

From its foundation centuries ago our old Cathedral had always been the church of St Michael; the new Cathedral being one building with the old, will remain under the same name. In his original design Mr Spence had placed a great figure of St Michael in bronze on the exterior wall overlooking the entrance to the porch, where all would see it. From the first he was determined that the only sculptor whom he would wish to see commissioned for this work was Sir Jacob Epstein, whom he regarded as unquestionably the greatest sculptor of this century.

In the summer of 1955, when the foundations of the new Cathedral were being laid, Mr Spence urged the Reconstruction Committee to commission Sir Jacob at once. He pointed out that Sir Jacob was now well into his seventies and might pass the zenith of his powers before we could employ him.

I felt it only right to remind the committee that many people, who did not understand Sir Jacob's work, found themselves repelled by it. Was there a danger that we might be placing in a position of inescapable prominence, at the door of the Cathedral, a statue that many of our church people would feel unable to accept? The committee asked me to go with Mr Spence to see Sir Jacob and report.

Accordingly, we went to see this very great man at his home in Kensington. I was immediately captured by his buoyant charm and vitality. He seemed to be immensely strong, physically, mentally and spiritually. The bronze head of a little child, a work of his that I saw in his studio was one of the most attractive sculptures I had ever seen. I had taken with me a short statement of what I believed to be the essential character of the archangel St Michael in his victory over the devil—sinless adoring vision of God, flashing brightness, strength and beauty, positive goodness, purity and love. Sir Jacob welcomed this description; and for my part I reported to the committee that we should banish all doubts, and that, if there was a risk, we should take it.

Bishop Neville Gorton in the last months of his life had been wholly in favour of commissioning Sir Jacob. He and I were easily able to win the approval of most of the Cathedral Council, but we felt it wise to compromise with the fears of the minority by asking Sir Jacob to present a preliminary design for consideration by the council.

Fifteen months passed, and we received no preliminary design from Sir Jacob. Early in 1957 we heard through the Press that he had already begun modelling the actual figure. When we enquired, Sir Jacob said that he was doing it for himself!

The new Bishop, Dr Cuthbert Bardsley, Mr Spence, Captain Thurston and I hastened to Sir Jacob's studio, and there we found that the work had indeed begun. The immense head, shoulders, and arms looked down from their height above us. We were spell-bound by the startling power and beauty of the head and face. More than all I had hoped for was expressed there—holiness, dedicated power, flashing vigour, poignant sorrow at the existence of evil. There was also a small model of the whole composition. I was overwhelmed with thankfulness that we had been led to commission Sir Jacob; I felt certain that when the figure should stand against the Cathedral wall, it would challenge young and old alike to enlist with the heavenly powers of holiness against the devilish attractions of evil. The Bishop admitted that he had gone to the studio in some trepidation but had been enthralled by the great physical beauty of the head and shoulders, the arresting face, and the strength and wisdom in the forehead. He had no hesitation in saying that it would be the greatest work that Sir Jacob had done. Needless to say, the Cathedral Council recorded their enthusiastic acceptance of the design.

Sir Jacob now worked on with the entire approval of his patrons. In twelve more months he had finished the group in plaster. It was placed on view for photography at the Morris Singer Works in London, where it was to be cast in bronze ready for setting up in its final position on the Cathedral wall between the porch and the baptistry windows (figure 17).

The Mural Panels

The conditions for the competition had asked that the eight "Hallowing Places", which for some years had proved such attractive and inspiring features of the ruins, should be reproduced in the new Cathedral. In Mr Spence's winning design the angled recesses between the walls and the windows had been intended for this purpose. On the eight wall spaces facing down towards the west end there were to be large sculptures corresponding to the eight spheres of human life symbolized by the Hallowing Places—work, home, education, art, etc.

The Bishop, Dr Neville Gorton, suggested that the sculptures should be scenes in the life of Jesus, each scene showing Our Lord fulfilling the activity of human life represented by that particular Hallowing Place. In the end, however, Mr Spence decided that the figure of Christ in the great tapestry should remain the only representation of Our Lord in the Cathedral.

Figure 17 "St. Michael and the Devil", in bronze, by Jacob Epstein, placed on the outside wall of the new Cathedral in 1960.

Next, Mr Spence suggested that the sculptures should not be pictorial representations, but should consist of words of Holy Scripture, incised on great stone panels at each Hallowing Place, and describing the action of Jesus Christ in the appropriate sphere of human life.

It was urged in some quarters that each Hallowing Place might suitably have an altar, so that it might be a side chapel for Holy Communion with special prayer for man's daily work in the sphere represented by that particular Hallowing Place. Mr Spence, however, felt that architecturally the multiplication of chapels on either side would detract from the central importance of the high altar; and the same objection was felt on ecclesiastical grounds.

At this point the new Bishop, Dr Cuthbert Bardsley, met the Provost and Chapter with a new inspiration, which eventually led to a different conception of the use of the eight recesses with their sculptures. The existing Hallowing Places in the ruins should become the permanent Hallowing Places of the Cathedral. The eight recesses in the new building should each have a stone panel; and these mural panels should be incised with words of Scripture, not necessarily connected with the Hallowing Places at all.

Mr Spence had already discovered a young sculptor named Ralph Beyer, whose lettering in stone he considered to be so outstanding that on his recommendation the Reconstruction Committee had commissioned him to inscribe the foundation stone in the new Cathedral. Mr Beyer's father had made a close study of the early Christian inscriptions in the catacombs, in which lettering and symbols are beautifully united. The results of his study had been embodied in an illustrated book. Mr Spence showed this book to the Bishop and myself, and suggested a similar treatment for the mural panels. We were so impressed that we arranged for Mr Beyer to produce a trial panel in stone; and when this was presented to the Committee, Chapter and

Council in September 1957, he was unanimously accepted as the designer of the eight mural panels.

The words and symbols to be inscribed on the panels were chosen by myself, as Provost; and the four Canons Theologian, Canons J. Ecclestone, J. H. Proctor, P. C. A. Carnegy, and N. S. Rathbone.

This was one of the most Important tasks of our lives. For centuries to come, the words would confront innumerable visitors to the Cathedral with the essential truths of the Christian Faith. We decided that the best choice would be the great sayings of Our Lord Himself, declaring who He is and what He came to do. Thus the Christ of the tapestry would speak through the Christ of the mural panels.

The words, we felt, must cover the eight most important aspects of Our Lord's Nature and Work, and must be chosen from the simpler texts of the Bible, so that "the wayfaring man" might understand. The final selection was approved by the Chapter in June 1958. The order proceeds from the west end of the Cathedral to the east, moving from side to side. The following texts and symbols were chosen:

I   "I and the Father are one ... He that hath seen me hath seen the Father."
Symbols: The sun, as expressing "Light of Light," and the ancient Christian Chi-Rho symbol (meaning "Christ").

II   "The Son of Man is come to seek and to save that which was lost ... The good shepherd giveth his life for the sheep."
Symbols : The good shepherd and a cross.

III "Come unto me all ye that labour and are heavy laden and I will give you rest. Take my yoke upon you, and learn of me; for I am meek and lowly in heart, and ye shall find rest unto your souls."
Symbol: A bold framing of the words.

IV "A new commandment I give unto you, that ye love one another, as I have loved you."
Symbol: Two hands showing wounds.

V   "Whoso eateth my flesh and drinketh my blood hath eternal life."

Symbols: Loaf and Chalice.

VI "When the Comforter is come, whom I will send unto you from the Father, even the spirit of Truth which proceedeth from the Father, he shall testify of me; and ye all shall bear witness."
Symbol: A bold framing of the words.

VII "I am the vine, ye are the branches, he that abideth in me and I in him, the same beareth much fruit; for apart from me ye can do nothing."
Symbol: The vine and branches.

VIII "Fear not; I am the first and the last ... I am, alive for Evermore, Amen; and have the keys of hell and of death."
Symbol: A key.

The Organ

As already recorded, the organ in the new Cathedral will be the gift of the people of Canada.

The organ of a cathedral is of great importance both as a work of musical art and also as an aid to divine worship. It was essential that we should provide an organ which would fulfil both these functions to the highest possible degree. Accordingly in June 1952 the Reconstruction Committee secured the services of three organists of repute as a body of advisers on the specifications of the new organ.

These advisers drew up specifications which were accepted by the committee.

The work of building the organ was entrusted to the firm of Harrison and Harrison, of Durham, whose head is Mr Cuthbert Harrison. In December 1953 the contract for building the organ was placed in a sum of £25,000.

CHAPTER TWELVE

—

Reconstruction in Progress, 1952-1958

FROM 1955 to 1956 Mr Spence held the Hoffman Wood professorship of architecture at Leeds University, and may conveniently be given the title in this chapter.

The work on the site of the new Cathedral began in June 1954, with the first preparations for the laying of the foundations. The three years before this date had been busy with essential preliminaries.

First, at the architect's headquarters, there was the elaborate work of making the exact drawings for the surveyors, who in turn would make the precise specifications to be presented to the builder. Until all the modifications to the design had been completed, which took several years, these drawings could not be begun. But by the middle of 1954 this stage had been settled as far as the foundations were concerned.

Soon after the announcement of the award in 1951 a large-scale model of the new Cathedral was constructed by the London City Display Organization. It covered a floor space of seven feet by five, and was accurate in every detail. It was enclosed in a glass case and equipped with interior lighting. After being prominently exhibited in the Royal Academy in 1952, it was placed in the exhibition under the tower of the Cathedral.

The model succeeded in arousing a new and wide interest in the design. Thousands were able for the first time to form an accurate impression in three dimensions of what the new Cathedral would really be like. While not all found the model to their liking, the added publicity was a help. A second model made in 1953, embodying the changes which had been made by that time, went right across Canada when Professor Spence * and I toured that country, and has since been shown in exhibitions in Britain and on the Continent.

But the chief advantage of these models is that they give the architect the opportunity of testing out accurately in three dimensions the aesthetic effects of his design. They are a necessary part of the preparation for actual reconstruction.

Before starting on the new Cathedral, Professor Spence had to see to the preservation of the ruins, which he was determined to retain as an integral part of his design. In accordance with his report, drawn up with the help of Mr Philip Chatwirt, work was begun on August 31st, 1952, after a service of dedication in the Wyley Crypt Chapel, attended by the staff and workmen of Messrs. J. R. Deacon Limited of Lichfield, the contractors.

The work of preservation was elaborate and very thorough. It embraced the sanctuary and all the walls of the ruins except the five north-east windows, which would abut on the new Cathedral porch. The walls were grouted throughout. Every stone in the face of the walls was carefully pointed with new mortar; where a stone had perished, it was replaced by a new stone. Along the top of the wall was placed a continuous concrete beam, rendering the walls completely waterproof. The tracery of the windows was repaired where it was weak or crumbling. In the case of the east window of the south aisle it was found necessary to remove all the tracery and to reproduce the window with entirely new stone. The work was completed by the end of 1954.

The total effect of this restoration was remarkable. The atmosphere of a ruin was unaltered, but the walls looked clean and cared for. Moreover, the visitors were now safe

---

* Spence was External Professor of Architecture at the University of Leeds from 1955 to 1957.

from falling bits of masonry, which had always been an anxiety before.

The Cappers' Room, above the south porch of the old Cathedral which adjoined the Cappers' Chapel, had traditionally belonged to the Cappers' Company, and they had used it for their annual meetings. In the great air raid it suffered badly; it lost its roof and its walls were badly scarred. The members of the Cappers' Guild, supported by Mr Ernest Ford, were anxious that this room might be restored in order to maintain the old-time connection of a City Guild with the Cathedral. The late Lord Iliffe, the Chairman of the Company, who had given generously to the first Cathedral appeal fund, asked that some of his gift might be spent on the restoration of their room.

In collaboration with Lord Iliffe, Professor Spence drew up specifications for the restoration, which was carried out by Messrs Deacon. The room was re-roofed, and the walls and tracery of the window completely restored. The Company have since equipped the room with a fine new refectory table and chairs, and a new tapestry, woven by Edinburgh Tapestry Company, depicting the arms of the Company. It is now one of the most beautiful meeting-rooms in the city. The room was dedicated by the Bishop at a service conducted by me in the presence of the whole Company on December 6th, 1957. The Company again have their annual meetings in it, and have made it available for the use of the Provost and staff of the Cathedral at their discretion. It has proved a very useful meeting place for small committees and interviews.

The Ministry of Works' licence for work on the new Cathedral was granted in May 1954. First we had to clear the graves from the graveyard, for it was upon this land that the west half of the new Cathedral was to be built. This necessitated building a fence right round the new Cathedral site. For this fence planning permission had to be obtained from the city authority; but this was forthcoming without delay and with the utmost goodwill. Speaking on behalf of the Planning and Redevelopment Committee: of the City Council, Alderman Hodgkinson, the Chairman, said that from a planning point of view the new Cathedral fitted beautifully into the central development of the city.

On June 8th, 1954, the first work on the site of the new Cathedral was begun by the digging by one of the workmen of the first sod for the erection of an oak fence to enclose the graveyard. To mark this epoch-making moment a short but very impressive Service of Hallowing was held, after which the work commenced.

First, the site of the west end of the new Cathedral and the Chapel of Unity was cleared of trees. It was with some sadness that we saw the great trees falling, but we were comforted by the reflection that a greater and more lasting beauty would take their place.

Then the human remains in the old disused graveyard were removed to consecrated ground farther away in the graveyard towards Holy Trinity Church. Screens were placed across the windows of the ruins, to prevent people watching. The work was gruesome, and we sympathized with the workmen who carried it out, but it was all done reverently and decently. It took many months to complete, but towards the end of autumn all was ready for the next stage.

In the autumn of 1954 the tender of Messrs John Laing and Sons Limited, was accepted for the first contract for laying the foundations up to and including the nave floor. It was not only very satisfying to know that we were putting our project into the hands of a firm renowned throughout the world for its high standards, but we also had the pleasure of knowing that Mr John Laing was a devout Christian (though not of the Church of England) who would dedicate himself with all of us to build to the glory of God.

At the same time Mr T. J. Hocking, formerly Chief Clerk of Works to the City Architect's Department in Plymouth was appointed our Clerk of Works. Mr Hocking also is a man of sincere Christian vocation, who felt himself called to this work of cathedral building. He has justified our hopes by his high degree of competence and his easy skill in personal relations.

The laying of the foundations was begun on March 7th, 1955. It was a tremendous operation, all traces of which are now covered up and out of sight under the Cathedral floor. It involved the removal of thousands of tons of soil to make way for the foundations of the nave.

Some 670 piles were driven into the ground, at a distance of two feet from each other, right round the lines of the walls to be built. These piles were made by boring holes fourteen inches in diameter and twenty to thirty feet deep until the rock was reached, and then filling this hole with concrete reinforced by four steel rods encircled by steel coils. Across these piles beams of reinforced concrete were built, and upon these the walls have since been raised. Each pile bears an average weight of fifty tons of wall.

The whole floor was laid out in reinforced concrete. Underneath the floor there is an elaborate system of ducts and corridors containing pipes and wires for the electric lighting and heating. At the east end, and along the whole length of the south side, there are amply-spaced undercrofts for the various uses of Cathedral administration (figure 18).

During the course of the excavation the east end of the ancient Coventry Cathedral was discovered, just overlapping the west wall of the new Cathedral. The part uncovered appears to be the base of a fourteenth century apse.

Meanwhile we suffered a sad loss. During 1955 Mr Ernest Ford had been in failing health, due largely to overwork. On November 15th he died, having accomplished a work for the new Cathedral for which we could not be too grateful. Through difficult years he had piloted the Committee, with calm wisdom in all emergencies and with friendly goodwill in all human relationships. His chairmanship will long be remembered by those who served with him.

**Figure 18 Four stages in THE BUILDING OF THE NEW CATHEDRAL
1956. The floor laid, with the undercroft beneath. The foundations
are out of sight beneath ground level. See p. 73.**

His successor as Chairman of the Reconstruction
Committee had been one of its regular members since its
creation in 1947. Colonel Sir Fordham Flower was not only
an experienced business man, but a personality well known
in Warwickshire, and a man of artistic interests. Shortly
before his own death Bishop Neville Gorton recommended
Colonel Flower to succeed Mr Ford. Colonel Flower accepted
the position, because he had a burning faith in the mission to
which we all felt pledged—to finish the building of the
Cathedral. He was pre-eminently the right man at the right
moment, for he had exactly the gifts required for carrying us
through the last stages of the reconstruction. There have
been critical moments when his faith and shrewd judgment
have been of the greatest value. He has been an admirable
leader of the reconstruction team.

Figure 19 Queen Elizabeth II in the ruins before the Laying of the Foundation Stone of the new Cathedral on March 23rd, 1956. With her are (l. to r.) the Provost, the Bishop, the Archbishop's cross-bearer and Canon Proctor.

On a gloriously sunny day, in the presence of a distinguished congregation, the foundation stone of the new Cathedral was laid by Her Majesty the Queen at a service on the site of the new Cathedral on March 23rd, 1956. (Figure 19). More than three thousand people, drawn from all our parishes, were seated in the nave of the new Cathedral which had been constructed up to floor level. The Queen's arrival was preceded by a procession of Free Church Ministers, including representatives of the German Evangelical Church, choirs of fifteen churches of the diocese, the Clergy and Readers of the Diocese of Coventry, and church dignitaries from other dioceses. Her Majesty accompanied by the Duke of Edinburgh, was attended by the Prime Minister and members of the Household, and escorted by the Lord Mayor and Lady Mayoress and the Town Clerk of Coventry, the Lord Lieutenant of Warwickshire and Lady Willoughby de Broke, the High Sheriff, and the Recorder of Coventry. The company entered the new Cathedral by the Queen's Way, which had been opened through the north wall of the Cathedral to give an approach from the old Cathedral to the floor of the new.

The service was overwhelming in its dignity and joy. The Lesson was read by a Free Church Minister, being the Vice-Chairman of the Joint Council in control of the Chapel of Unity; the new Bishop of Coventry, Dr Cuthbert Bardsley, gave the address; the Queen, receiving a mallet and trowel from Professor Spence, laid the Foundation Stone with the accustomed ceremonies; the Archbishop of Canterbury blessed the Stone; the Provost led the prayers of dedication. The Cathedral bells and a fanfare of trumpets marked the arrival and departure of the Queen, as though rejoicing in this great occasion.

Directly the foundations were finished, a second contract was made with Messrs J. Laing for facing the walls of the foundation from ground to floor level with the pink-grey sandstone with which the Cathedral was to be built. The stone comes from Messrs Stanton and Bettoney's "Two Gates" quarry at Hollington in Staffordshire. It was estimated that the Cathedral would eventually require twenty-seven thousand stones. Professor Spence decided to make use only of pink stone mottled with white patches, because mottled stone was coming out of the quarries in greater quantities than plain pink stone, and because it gave a more varied and interesting surface. The process of facing was finished by the autumn of 1956.

One problem which Professor Spence has considered with especial care is that of acoustics. In a great cathedral it is essential that both speech and music should be heard clearly and without reverberation. Much research has recently been done on this problem; and Professor Spence has kept constantly in touch with the Government Research Station obtaining their practical advice at every stage of the work.

And now began the long-awaited work—the building of the walls. The third contract with Messrs Laing, in a sum of £791,000, was signed on December 13th, 1956. Earlier in the day special prayers had been offered at Holy Communion for the Cathedral project and for all the people concerned with it; and when the contract was signed the Bishop prayed for divine blessing on the work. This was a day we had been eagerly waiting for.

The work of building the walls began in February 1957, and continued without interruption. As the walls rose we became conscious, first of the great size of the building, then of the beauty of the windows, then of the harmonious composition of the wall masses, seen singly or together. By the end of 1958 the walls were up to the roof level, and the Cathedral-to-be had begun to appear (figure 20) a solid reality in the midst of the city and diocese.

Figure 20 1959. The nave walls built up to roof level.

The Dean and Chapter of Lichfield Cathedral offered us a stone taken from their ancient building, to be incorporated into our new Cathedral. We gladly accepted this offer, and the stone was built into the west wall, at the north side of the glass screen. By the presence of this stone at the heart of the fabric of our new Cathedral we are united with the glorious tradition of our sister Cathedral at Lichfield, and of all the ancient cathedrals of Christendom.

CHAPTER THIRTEEN

—

*The Continuing Life of the
Cathedral, 1943-1958*

WE must now pick up the story of the Cathedral ruins
where we left it at the end of Chapter five, after Alamein
Victory Sunday at the end of 1942.

The Removal of the Rubble and the New Look

For five more years the piles of rubble remained. We
could not get permission to remove them, because of
wartime restrictions on labour. This was not wholly
regretted, as many people felt that the rubble was what gave
the ruins their power, and this power might vanish if the
rubble was cleared. For the rest of the war the ruins
continued to inspire, challenge, and comfort the tired spirits
of Coventry.

Then, in the spring of 1948, a striking change took place.
As has already been recorded, the rubble was removed, and
the Cathedral ruins took on their new look, which has now
become familiar. It is remarkable that this happened almost
simultaneously with the mission of forgiveness from
Coventry to Kiel in Germany, which is described later in this
chapter. So far from the power of the ruins vanishing, their
message was made stronger by four important new
elements.

Hitherto, in the sanctuary, there had only been the Altar of
Rubble and the Charred Cross. Now a large silver-plated
Cross of Nails was placed on the altar, standing on a stone
pedestal at the base of the Charred Cross. On the walls of the
sanctuary behind the altar were carved the two words

"Father forgive", in huge letters that could be read a long way off. The contrast between the black Charred Cross and the silvered Cross of Nails was eloquent of the message of life out of death, and the words on the wall preached the gospel of divine forgiveness as movingly as any human voice could do.

On a tall pedestal against the wall, just outside the sanctuary, was placed a life-size figure of Christ, which had been modelled in clay before the war by a Blundell's School boy of seventeen, and cast in plaster. He had joined the R.A.F. and been killed. Looking down, with welcoming hands spread out, the figure made a strong appeal to all who saw it.

In the Chapel of the Resurrection an ebony crucifix carved by an eighteen-year-old African boy, was hung on the wall opposite the altar. The beauty of the carving, the evident suffering of the body, the simple dignity of the face made this crucifix a veritable missionary from Africa, proclaiming the love of the Saviour of mankind.

Hallowing Places

Eight "Hallowing Places" were set round the walls of the ruins. These are small enclosures, open to the sky, about four feet by six, surrounded by a wall one foot high on which flowers grow. Each "Hallowing Place" has a board on the Cathedral wall facing it, with two prayers. For instance, the Hallowing Place of the Home was "Hallowed be thy name in the Horne" and "God be in my heart and in my loving"; and there are similar prayers for work, education, the arts, commerce, government, recreation and suffering.

Their meaning and purpose is extremely simple. Each Hallowing Place represents some part of the daily life of Everyman as he lives it out in the world. At that spot, by means of the words on the board, he is helped to remember that this aspect of his daily life, like every other, is sacred to God, and that God must be worshipped in it as much as in church. Since each Hallowing Place leads up to the High Altar (each being really a part of the sanctuary of that one altar), he realizes that his life, at home, at work, at play, is to be brought to the altar and offered up to God in the Eucharist, and that his worship at the altar gives him the power to make his life in the world a continual worship.

These Hallowing Places are a modern development of the ancient guild chapels that used to stand around the interior of the old Cathedral. They have added greatly to the interest of the ruins, and have been a source of inspiration to thousands of people.

In 1946, as the number of visitors increased, we realized we must find some way of looking after them. We therefore appointed Mrs Browett as a lady steward, later joined by Miss Allen. They soon came to know the Cathedral, the ruins and the chapels intimately, and they passed on their knowledge to the visitors. Most days of the week they were in the Cathedral all day long. Their lay ministry, for such it has been, lasted many years, and greatly contributed to the life of the Cathedral.

Canon Proctor

After being alone at the Cathedral from its destruction until 1946, I had the good fortune to be able to make what I always feel to have been the best appointment of my life. Canon J. H. Proctor*, who was vicar of a parish in the diocese Leicester, responded to my invitation to join me in my work, and came as Precentor of the Cathedral. He at once entered fully into the spirit of the Cathedral, and gave himself with complete devotion to seizing the great opportunities for serving God and the people which the Cathedral offered. For twelve years we worked together as colleagues, and almost everything that I have done in the Cathedral was done in the closest collaboration with him and with his most wise advice.

A new guide to the Cathedral was now produced, bringing the description of the ruins up to date, and explaining the

---

* Archdeacon of Warwick from 1958

meaning of their various parts. A series of five pamphlets on "The Message of Coventry Cathedral" was jointly produced by Canon Proctor and myself. The usual picture postcards were made available. An exhibition of pictures was opened under the tower.

Daily And Sunday Services

"A Cathedral is built not primarily to be looked at but to be prayed in"—how often has that been said to visitors. "And do you have any services in the Cathedral?" they often asked. The answer was that we do that which every Cathedral is built for: we make the continual offering of prayer to God Most High.

Throughout those twelve post-war years, every weekday morning (except Thursdays and Holy Days) prayer was offered in the Chapel of the Resurrection for the needs of the people of the diocese, and for the city, and for the Cathedral visitors. The Bishop and clergy, the Lord Mayor and Corporation, and all the multifarious activities of the community, were all held up in prayer before God.

In particular, daily year after year the reconstruction of the Cathedral was laid before God as we asked His guidance and help. Through the difficult days of controversy and perplexity, and through the bright days of progress and achievement, the planners and designers, the architects and craftsmen, the stonemasons and labourers were daily named before God. The dogged perseverance and the brilliant inspiration that have resulted in the Cathedral rising before our eyes are due to God's good Providence granted in answer to prayer offered daily in the Cathedral.

Every week-day evening in the Chapel of the Resurrection Evensong was said, that deeply moving offering of the Church's liturgical worship, which reaches its peak in the Magnificat, the song of joy of the Mother of Our Lord at the Incarnation. At this service every diocese of the Anglican Communion throughout the world (there are more than 300 of them) was named in turn before God in prayer, in union with other cathedral churches where the same cycle of prayer is used.

A cathedral church has a mission to fulfil, not only to the Cathedral city, but to the whole diocese. During those post-war years the Cathedral was able to make an increasing impact upon the life of the diocese. A Residentiary Canonry was established, so that a full-time Canon might work in the diocese under the direction of the Bishop and join in the "Continual Offering of Prayer" in the Cathedral. In this capacity from 1951 to 1958 Canon E. Moore Darling went widely through the parishes taking missions, and did a notable work in the factories of Coventry as an industrial chaplain. From 1946 to 1958, at the request of the Bishop Canon Proctor undertook a recruitment campaign for ordination candidates, which achieved a success unique among the dioceses of England. As Chaplain of the Cathedral from 1954 to 1958, Canon Bennett got to know many people in the factories, and worked to create a new link between Industry and the Church. It fell to my lot to be the chairman of the Diocesan Missionary Council, which is the instrument of the diocese for the spreading of the Christian Faith overseas; and also of the Coventry and Warwickshire Association for the Deaf, which ministers to the spiritual and social needs of the deaf people of the diocese.

Pilgrims and Visitors

Meanwhile the ruins of the Cathedral continued their own missionary work on visitors from all over the world.

I have already referred to the strange power that the ruins exercise on the hearts and minds of those who see them. Visitors came in greater numbers each year, and most of them went away deeply impressed. The beauty of the walls the green and peaceful aisles and lawns, the tragic and triumphant scene at the sanctuary, the sight through the ruined window of the rising new Cathedral, and not least the three Chapels—the Chapel of the Resurrection, the Crypt Chapel of Eucharistic Worship, and the temporary Chapel of Unity—all these things together struck deep into the heart.

Canon Proctor, the stewards, and I myself were constantly taking individuals or groups round the ruins and into the chapels, where we would, try to interpret to them the inward meaning of the many things they saw. We always found that something gripped them and inspired them, though few could find words for what it was. Those who were able to put their thoughts into words told us that they had been tremendously helped and challenged, comforted and healed in spirit. We believe that what happened was that they heard the voice of God.

Most of these visitors came singly or in small family groups. They were of every occupation and all ages—there were many children, and many teenagers in every kind of sporting clothes. During the summer we had great numbers of visitors from the Commonwealth, and from countries all over the world.

Sometimes particularly distinguished people would pay us a formal visit. The ambassadors of many countries honoured us in this way, sometimes with their wives: Chile, Brazil, the U.S.A., Czechoslovakia, Germany, the Netherlands and Yugoslavia were thus represented. There were forty African chiefs, who took a poignant interest in the ebony crucifix—the African Christ. A Canon of Kampala Cathedral in Uganda, a very saintly African Christian, was photographed at the high altar holding with me a Cross of Nails. A priest of the Church of South India brought us a brass offertory bowl as a present from his Cathedral Church in Dornakal. A Chinese priest, now bishop, celebrated Holy Communion in the Crypt Chapel in an unforgettable voice of Christian prayerfulness. Field Marshal Lord Montgomery was told how the bells had rung out on Alamein Victory Sunday.

Our Queen paid her first visit to the Cathedral in 1948, as Princess Elizabeth. She was then twenty-two. At that early age she revealed herself as a woman of happy charm, serious dignity, and sensitive understanding. At the High Altar I gave her a tiny plated Cross of Nails, telling her that it was the most precious thing we had to give. Her visit to lay the foundation stone of the new Cathedral is recorded in Chapter twelve.

In 1951 King George VI and Queen Elizabeth came, he for the third time, she for the second. It was within a year of the King's death. He struck me forcibly by his quiet and friendly dignity. If even then, as Sir Winston Churchill was afterwards to say, he was "walking with Death", he seemed to me to be already "walking with God".

In 1957 Princess Margaret made a brief tour of the ruins came down into the Chapel of Unity, accepted a Cross of Nails, and was taken round the new Cathedral by the architect.

In 1958 the Duchess of Kent paid her second visit, in order to see the building of the new Cathedral. She told me that she still kept by her bedside the Cross of Nails that I had given her fourteen years before.

Some of our visitors have come to Coventry on pilgrimage. We have encouraged parties of people from parishes, schools, clubs and societies in the diocese to make this pilgrimage to their own Cathedral Church. They have come from mothers' unions, youth fellowships, men's societies, Sunday schools, day schools, of the Anglican and Free Church communions. Likewise, similar groups from outside the diocese have made their long journey of pilgrimage to Coventry Cathedral. In all cases the pilgrimage has ended with a service or act of prayer.

Great Services

A Cathedral Church is built to accommodate a very great number of people, so that from time to time God may be worshipped there by large congregations, thus expressing the fellowship of all Christian people in the family of Christ.

The ruins were able to perform this function, though they were completely exposed to the weather. Large-scale services were held in the ruins, especially after the rubble had been removed. Sometimes it rained, and the service would have to be transferred to the ready hospitality of Holy Trinity Church. But usually the weather was kind, and then no setting for a service could be more beautiful, with the sky above, the sun bringing out the colours of the stone walls, the open tracery of the windows, and the birds flitting overhead.

On a March morning in 1944 President Benes of Czechoslovakia came with the Czech Army Choir for a service entitled "Lidice Shall Live", held in the ruins in commemoration of the martyrdom of the Czech village of Lidice.

On V.E. Day, May 8th, 1945, the people of Coventry completely took possession of the ruins, by day and by night. The sanctuary was set out with the flags of all the allied nations, and massed with flowers. A bowl on the altar received the names of the fallen. Short services of thanksgiving were held throughout the day. But it was at night, and far on after midnight, that the people crowded in, walked up to the floodlit sanctuary, and stood silently before the altar with its Crosses, until tens of thousands had paid their spontaneous tribute of thanksgiving and commemoration.

Mrs Gorton, the Bishop's wife, said to me, "Provost, talk to them." So I stood in the sanctuary, holding in my hands the Cross of Nails from the altar; and talked to party after party as they streamed up and back.

The Colours of the 7th Battalion, The Royal Warwickshires, had been placed in the Cathedral in October 1939 and I have described in Chapter three how they were rescued from the fire. On November 7th, 1948, they were brought to the Cathedral and formally returned to the Battalion, in the presence of a large congregation. On June 4th, 1961, they were taken to St Mary's Church, Warwick, and in the presence of Field Marshal Viscount Montgomery were laid up in the regimental chapel of the Battalion. It is planned that they shall finally be laid up in the Chapel of the Cross under the new Cathedral.

The Festival of Britain was celebrated in the Cathedral by a gathering of the united choirs of the Church of England and the Free Churches, with the City of Coventry Band in their midst. A thousand singers and a congregation of the same size joined in this joyful festival of music. Hymns and anthems were sung, the work of British authors and composers of several centuries, and the congregation joined in prayers. The Mayor of Coventry, Councillor Harry Weston was the leading spirit of the Festival.

Some great diocesan services maintained the tradition that the Cathedral is the natural rallying place of the diocesan family. In the Festival Year, 1951, there fell also 250th anniversary of the founding of the Society for the Propagation of the Gospel. In the morning of June 17th this anniversary was celebrated in the ruins by a Choral Eucharist, to which people came from all the parishes of the diocese. The Bishop was the celebrant, and the sermon was preached by the Rt. Rev. F. S. Hollis, formerly Bishop of Labuan and Sarawak. A male voice choir, based on the Cathedral choir led the singing of the Communion Service and the hymns.

The conclusion of the Laymen's Appeal, which had run for five years, was marked by a Diocesan Gift Day in the ruins on April 23rd, 1955. Churchwardens and laity from the parishes brought their final gifts, and presented them to the Bishop. When the day closed, the fund had reached £108,000, which was £3,000 beyond the target. The day began with Holy Communion in the West Crypt, and closed with Evensong in the ruins.

The coronation of Queen Elizabeth II was marked by civic services in the Cathedral on Coronation Sunday, May 30th, and especially by a youth service in the ruins, organized by the Diocesan Youth Council. Six hundred young people between the ages of fifteen and twenty-five came from more than ninety parishes. The address was given by Bishop Frank Woods, afterwards Archbishop of Melbourne.

On a warm March afternoon in 1950 the daughter of Captain Thurston was married by the Provost in the Cathedral ruins, in the presence of a large congregation. The Bishop gave the blessing. An orchestra provided the music, and a church choir led the singing. The setting was unique, and the service very beautiful and impressive.

May 8th, 1955, the tenth anniversary of V.E. Day, was marked by a great service of community hymn-singing in the ruins in the evening, attended by more than a thousand people from the three Anglican congregations of the Cathedral, Christ Church and St Thomas' Church, and of the three Free Church congregations of Warwick Road Congregational Church, Queen's Road Baptist Church and the Central Hall Methodist Church. The hymns were introduced by the Provost, the Precentor and the Free Church ministers.

Certain services were repeated year after year. Five of these stand out as worthy of special record. In April, on St George's Day Sunday, the Cathedral would be filled with nearly two thousand scouts and cubs from the district. In July King Henry VIII School would invite parents and old boys to celebrate its Founder's Day. In early September eight hundred old-age pensioners would come for an old people's service. On Battle of Britain Sunday the Royal Air Force Association would come, with R.A.F. contingents from stations in the diocese. On Christmas Eve in the floodlit ruins, with braziers burning and illuminated Christmas trees there would always be hundreds of people—sometimes more than a thousand—singing the familiar Christmas carols, led by the boys and young men of the Coventry School of Music band.

Drama in the Ruins

Coventry was once famous for the open-air performance of its mystery plays, and the Cathedral ruins were an obvious place to stage some of the religious dramas that have been produced in recent years. During the war, before the rubble had been removed, three dramatic events were held, the audience sitting mainly on the rubble itself as there was not room for many chairs. In 1944 a Coventry amateur company put on a play by T. B. Morris, specially written with reference to the ruins, and representing the fight between St Michael and the Devil for the soul of Man. In 1945 another amateur company performed T. S. Eliot's "Murder in the Cathedral". That same year Mr Tom Harrison, of the Council for the Encouragement of Music and the Arts produced a pageant of the history of the Church in Coventry from the eleventh century to the present time. It was organized by the Friends of Coventry Cathedral, and hundreds of actors from church and civic dramatic groups took part. The performances were floodlit, as they were held at night, and acted on a high stage right across the east end of the Cathedral.

There was another period of dramatic activity between 1949 and 1952. The rubble had now been removed. In 1949 the fourth centenary of the First English Prayer Book was celebrated by a Prayer Book Pageant, composed by Canon Proctor and acted in the ruins on a summer evening by actors from many parishes, to an audience of two thousand.

In 1949 an open-air stage, designed by Mr Charles Thomas of the British Drama League, was built against the north wall of the Cathedral, the cost being borne by the Friends of Coventry Cathedral. A whole series of plays was performed on this stage for four years running. The climax was reached in the Festival year, when for nearly a month on end there were performances every weekday of the celebrated Coventry Guild Plays. The producer, Miss Carina Robins of the Religious Drama Society, drew her cast from local church and industrial drama groups. The City Council, and many local firms, organizations, and citizens helped to meet the cost. The result was a production that played a worthy part in the Festival of Britain.

Bequest and Gifts

Before the war, Coventry Cathedral had been poorly endowed; but in 1948 the late Lord Kenilworth, formerly Sir John Siddeley, the founder of the Armstrong Siddeley Motor Works, made the munificent gift of £100,000 for the endowment of the Cathedral, which received this benefaction with the utmost gratitude. It is to come into use when the Cathedral is open for services, and will be available for the maintenance of the fabric, and for the support of the clergy, choir and vergers. This gift, which will be administered by the Church Commissioners, will relieve the Cathedral of most of its former anxiety about money. Never has so large a sum from the proceeds of industry been ploughed back into the spiritual resources of the people, and never has the Church in Coventry received so generous and imaginative a gift.

When the Cathedral was destroyed, it lost almost all its possessions. Gradually new gifts of ornaments and furniture have been presented, most of which will pass over into the use of the new Cathedral. Two gift sets of Communion Plate, a Georgian one of silver and a modern one of glass, have been added to the four sets which survived the destruction. Five churchwarden's staves of ebony, mounted with silver mitre and crosses, were given just in time for the laying of the Foundation Stone. A new processional cross was presented in 1953 by the Dowager Marchioness of Reading, in memory of the war service of the Women's Voluntary Services for Civil Defence; it was beautifully designed by Mr Leslie Durbin, and made in Perspex, silver and gold. It was dedicated at a service on Ascension Day, attended by five hundred members of the W.V.S. (figure 21). A public subscription in memory of Colonel Sir William Wyley provided completely new oak furniture for the Wyley Crypt Chapel in 1951, and his relations gave the silver altar cross.

Figure 21 The service in the ruins on May 14th, 1953, for the dedication of the processional cross given in memory of the W.V.S. fallen.

German Contacts

Of all the visitors to the Cathedral ruins, none seem more profoundly moved than those from Germany, young and old alike. This appears to have grown out of two events that happened just after the war.

The Christmas Empire Broadcast of 1946 opened with an interchange of Christian greetings between me, in the temporary Chapel of Unity with some English children, and a Roman Catholic priest in Hamburg with some German children, the children singing the verse of a carol after our words of greeting. It was the first time since the war that there had been such mutual fellowship in public between Britain and Germany. In the course of my greeting I said:

> You know what happened to us here in Coventry, and you can easily picture what it was like. We know what happened to you in Hamburg, and can partly imagine it ...
> I think I see between us at our feet, the Christ Child lying in His crib. Across the Child I stretch out my hand and put it into

yours, my brother. Looking down into the face of the infant Jesus—God in human flesh—two words spring to my lips to say to you. The first word is "Forgiveness"...

The second word is this—"New Birth". Here in Coventry we have 20,000 new homes to build, a whole new city centre and a Cathedral to restore. Your task is even greater. But more important still, there is a new spirit to be born—new courage, new faith, new unselfishness, new pity for each other's sufferings, new family love and purity.

The reply of Pastor Mecklenburg came clearly through:

I hear your voice, my brother of Coventry, and thank you for your Christian understanding. The ruins of Hamburg lie all around me. Mile after mile of desolation. Fifty per cent of our houses are destroyed and half the remainder damaged ... The struggle for existence here is desperate ...

Never before has Christ been such a reality in our midst. We experience Him in this hour as a light which leads us home and brings us new light and new hope for a new future.

Your message of forgiveness and new birth awakens an echo in my heart. "Forgive us our trespasses as we forgive them that trespass against us." If only those words could be echoed in all hearts! If only we could cast out bitterness and hatred and begin again, then I believe that our children—yours and ours—may live together in peace and brotherhood.

In 1947 an invitation came from the Oberburgomaster of Kiel in Germany, for a mission of friendship to go from Coventry to that city, the base of German submarine warfare. Coventry sent the Mayor, a trade union official, and myself as representing the Churches. It fell to me to speak at a large meeting of Christians, Protestant and Roman Catholic. I assured them of our wish for Christ's sake to forgive and be forgiven all mutual injuries, and in token of this I gave to the Provost of their wholly destroyed Cathedral a small Cross of Nails. Next day he took me to the ruins of his Cathedral and gave me a small piece of stone from the rubble, as a reciprocal symbol of forgiveness. This stone I brought back to Coventry and placed in the Chapel of Unity. It is called "The Kiel Stone of Forgiveness".

During the late forties the trickle of visitors from Germany to the Cathedral began to increase. During the fifties it became a steady stream. I took every opportunity of showing them round. At the sanctuary they would look at the words "Father forgive". In the Chapel of Unity I would put the Cross of Nails into their hands and assure them that the Cross of Christ annihilates the guilt of sinful man. I would tell them the story of the Kiel Stone. Again and again the spiritual miracle would happen. Germans still bound in the fetters of war guilt would be suddenly set free, and would go away with a new sense of release and tranquil joy.

In the early fifties Pastor Kurtz, the German Lutheran Pastor for the Midlands, began to take Lutheran services in the Chapel of Unity for German Lutherans resident in Coventry. I found him a man possessed with a radiant spirit of Christian charity and joy. It was largely through his initiative that a movement sprang up among the Christian Churches of Germany to raise the cost of the stained-glass windows in the Chapel of Unity. Dr Heuss, President of the Federal German Republic, took a personal interest in this movement. On President Heuss's seventieth birthday, in January 1954, Pastor Kurtz and I conducted a service of thanksgiving and prayer on the President's behalf in the Chapel of Unity, attended by the Bishop, the Lord Mayor and a mixed English and German congregation.

The money for the windows was raised by 1958. President Heuss brought it over to London during his visit to Britain in October, and presented it to the new Provost of Coventry.

Meanwhile there had been another remarkable instance of German generosity. In April 1958 I was unexpectedly invited to visit the German Embassy in London, to receive from the hands of Dr Adenauer, the Chancellor of the German Republic, a gift for the Coventry Cathedral Reconstruction

Fund. Dr Adenauer, who is a Roman Catholic received me very graciously and presented me with a cheque in German marks that was the equivalent of £4,250. He said that he gave it "as a German and as a Christian". I replied that I received it with deep gratitude "as an Englishman and as a Christian". It was made clear that the gift was from the German Government. Subsequently, in acknowledging a Cross of Nails I had sent him, he said that the gift had been "an expression of the wish of the German people to help make good what a ruthless régime destroyed". It only remains to record that at the laying of the foundation stone of the new Cathedral in 1956 a representative body of the German Evangelical Church joined the procession of Free Church Ministers and took part in the service, thus sealing our mutual forgiveness and fellowship in the One Body of Christ.

The Death of Doctor Neville Gorton

On November 30th, 1955, Dr Neville Gorton, Lord Bishop of Coventry since 1943, died at the age of sixty-seven after a very short and unexpected illness. At the funeral service in Holy Trinity Church, attended by the Lord Mayor and Corporation and the Lord Lieutenant of Warwickshire, Dr Fisher, Archbishop of Canterbury, gave the address, and paid a moving tribute to the great spiritual powers of Dr Gorton whom he had known since school days. The Bishop was buried in the ruins, at the far south-east corner of the Cathedral, just outside the sanctuary. A beautiful gravestone now stands there as the permanent memorial to a great Bishop.

Dr Neville Gorton will ever be remembered in the city and diocese for his loving charity towards all people. It is universally recognized that in this he followed closely in the steps of Our Lord Jesus Christ, the great Shepherd of the souls of men.

Throughout the thirteen years of his episcopate Dr Gorton had the deepest interest in his Cathedral Church. His ideal for a Cathedral was that it should be not only a building for Anglican worship of the highest order, but both an instrument of compassionate service to the struggling multitudes of the city and diocese, and also a centre of Christian charity. Thus the scheme for a Cathedral Christian Service Centre was largely his idea. He fully supported the plan to make a Chapel of Unity in the new Cathedral, and approved of our making a temporary Chapel of Unity in the Crypt under the ruins.

The Enthronement of Doctor Cuthbert Bardsley

On May 5th, 1956, Dr Cuthbert Bardsley was enthroned in the ruins at a great service attended by two thousand people from all parts of the diocese, and from the parishes at Croydon, Southwark and Woolwich, which he had formerly served, Dr Bardsley had already been present to give the address at the laying of the Foundation Stone. Like Dr Gorton, the new Bishop was wholly in favour of the new Cathedral design, and he wanted the reconstruction done quickly. He urged that, while the War Damage Commission payment might go a long way to defray the cost, it was only right that the people should want to contribute a good share. Taking up a suggestion of two Coventry business men, he launched the scheme for a Festival of Coventry Cathedral at the time of the Consecration in 1962. It was due to his wisdom and determination that his tremendous appeal for half a million pounds for the diocese should be inseparably united with an appeal for half that sum for the reconstruction of the Cathedral (see Chapter eighteen).

Canadian Generosity

The Cathedral owes much to the generosity of Canada. Shortly after the end of the war I received a letter from Dr Healey Willan, Chairman of the Canadian College of Organists, saying that the College wished to raise a sum of money from the choirs and organists of Canada as a contribution to the organ in our new Cathedral. The name of Healey Willan gave me the greatest pleasure, since, before the destruction one of his settings of the Magnificat had been a great favourite with the Cathedral choir. He came to England and made a great impression on us, and was himself deeply attracted by what he saw of the Cathedral. In due course a cheque for more than £10,000 was received from Canada, which, along with the War Damage Commission compensation for the loss of the old organ, will pay for the excellent new organ which is to be installed. The instrument can thus be called the gift of Canada.

In 1952 Dr R. S. K. Seeley, Provost of Trinity College, Toronto, visited Coventry, where he had been ordained in the Cathedral twenty years before. We were planning an appeal to Canada, and Dr Seeley gave us reason to hope that there might be a response of as much as £25,000. Accordingly Mr Spence and myself were commissioned to go in the autumn of 1953 with the Bishop's Chaplain, the Rev. C. E. Ross, as the organizer of our tour.

For three months we toured right across Canada, telling the story of the destruction of the old Cathedral and our plans for the new. Throughout the journey we received the warmest possible welcome. Mr Spence lectured on the new Cathedral and aroused the interest of hundreds of architects. Mr Ross and I preached in many churches, including some of the United Church of Canada. To each church I preached in, including six cathedrals, I presented a Cross of Nails which was received with appreciation and gratitude. We promised that the Canadian symbol of the maple leaf should find a place in the floor of the new Cathedral. In the end the appeal realized £22,000, and we were assured that our visit had been highly successful as a mission of goodwill.

Once the building operations had begun, in 1955, we were able to take visitors on to the floor and show them the new Cathedral actually coming into being. It was now possible to describe on the spot the future beauties of the baptistry window, the nave windows, the altar, the tapestry, the murals, and make them visualize the completed Cathedral far better than they could imagine it from guide books and pictures.

In the year 1957 an interesting modification was made in the constitution of the Cathedral as a parish church cathedral. Owing mainly to the redevelopment of the city centre the once large population of the parish of St Michael had not only shrunk in size but had lost its cohesion and connection with the Cathedral at its centre. The various outlying parts of the parish were therefore for their own good transferred to the adjoining parishes. The Cathedral, however, kept a small area round itself as the parish of St Michael, in this way retaining the advantages of being a parish of the deanery of Coventry.

The Friends of the Cathedral

This chapter can be brought to a fitting climax by describing the faithful work of the Friends of Coventry Cathedral. During most of this period they have been a small body, scattered throughout the diocese with a strong nucleus at Coventry, dedicated to the love and support of their Mother Church. It was they who provided the Chapel of the Resurrection, the open-air stage, the tablets for the Hallowing Places, and a magnificent cope made by the Royal School of Needlework for the laying of the foundation stone. In 1957 a "Chief Friend" was appointed in most of the parishes of the diocese, and so successfully did these new leaders recruit help that by 1958 the total number of Friends had risen to a thousand. It is an inestimable boon to the Cathedral to have this large company of supporters in all parts of the diocese. As the new Cathedral approaches completion, it is they who kindle the interest of their fellow-church-people, and prepare them for the day of its Consecration.

CHAPTER FOURTEEN

—

The Cathedral Congregation in the West Crypt, 1946-1958

PRIMARILY a church is not a building, but people. This is as true for a Cathedral as for a parish church. The body of people who regularly worship and serve God in the Cathedral building keep this building spiritually warm, not only for themselves, but for the thousands who come from: all over the diocese to attend special diocesan services, and for the Cathedral's innumerable visitors. These people are the Cathedral congregation.

For the first five years after the destruction the Cathedral congregation were the guests of Holy Trinity Church. By the end of 1945 the West Crypt, the larger of the two crypts under the Cathedral, had been completely restored and dedicated as the temporary Chapel of Unity (see page 51). Accordingly, the Cathedral congregation was transferred at the beginning of 1946, and held its services there for twelve years. The chapel is perhaps the most beautiful mediaeval building in Coventry; but it can only hold a hundred people, and therefore could not accommodate a large congregation. Holy Communion was celebrated in the neighbouring Wyley Crypt Chapel, which could be seen from the West Crypt through two unglazed windows. We realized that it would be a long time before a full-sized congregation could be assembled in the new Cathedral; for the time being we must remain a small congregation, and try to discover some way of worship and life together that might be an example and inspiration to the other churches of the diocese. Only thus could we be a Cathedral congregation in any true sense. As was recorded in Chapter five the Holy Communion was celebrated in the Wyley Crypt Chapel early every Sunday morning from the time of the destruction. This continued to be the weekly Eucharist of the Cathedral congregation.

It was at this point that Canon Proctor joined me as Precentor of the Cathedral. On the weekdays we were incessantly busy with the daily services in the chapels, with the pilgrimages in the ruins, and with Cathedral and diocesan work. On alternate Sundays we went out preaching in the churches of the diocese, carrying the greetings and message of the mother church to the parishes. But we jointly took pastoral care of the congregation, taking care to be together from time to time at the Sunday services, and almost always being together at the celebrations of Holy Communion. Over the twelve years there grew up between the two of us and the congregation an unusually close bond, and the burden of work for Canon Proctor and myself was greatly lightened by the prayers and fellowship of the congregation.

It appeared to us that one of the weaknesses of our present-day practice of churchgoing was the absence of families, of fathers and mothers and children all coming together. We decided to make eleven o'clock Mattins our family service. Some people regard Mattins as a dull service; but it can be a very joyful and interesting act of worship, and one that children thoroughly enjoy. Moreover, we decided that children should grow up familiar with the Church of England services, and not merely with some special form of children's service, however good it might be occasionally. By choosing suitable hymns, introducing suitable biddings and explanations, and selecting lessons within the compass of a child's understanding, occasionally using a simpler word in place of a difficult one, we made the service enjoyable even for quite little children. At the sermon the children went out in two groups (up to seven and over seven) to the nearby chapels for special talks. Fifteen to twenty minutes later they came back to join their families again.

Once a month the service would be Choral Communion—choral to the extent of hymns. This was the monthly Eucharistic consummation of our Sunday morning worship. The younger children went to their classes after the creed, but when they neared the age of Confirmation they stayed throughout the service; and all stayed at the greater festivals.

The result of this experiment was that gradually the congregation came to consist predominantly of young parents with families of one to five children, all joining in the service with obvious enjoyment. The older members of the congregation welcomed the arrival of families. There were many who discovered that they could worship God better as adults because of the presence of young people and children.

The surviving members of the old Cathedral Choir formed themselves into a new choir, augmented by other singers of both sexes. In such a confined space it inevitably became the chief function of the choir to lead the singing of the congregation, and they did this very well, to the great benefit of the worship. At the same time they trained themselves to render works of Church music from time to time.

The choristers now grown to manhood, with the younger ladies, created an independent choir of younger singers, mainly students, calling themselves the Vacation Choir. Cherishing the ideals they had imbibed as boys from their celebrated choirmaster, Alan Stephenson, they courageously aimed at the high standard of singing of a cathedral choir. Their renderings of Choral Evensong impressed people with high standards in musical matters, and their skill and devotion were a fine tribute to the glory of God.

At the heart of the congregation were the five Cathedral churchwardens. They were the backbone of the administrative life of the congregation, and the personal friends of all. Mr P. G. Loveitt (died in 1959) was a greatly loved and respected citizen of Coventry, who remained Provost's Warden until he was more than ninety years old. With him as People's Wardens were Mr A. E. Jeffers (died in

1960). Mr G.J.T. Collier, Mr A. E. Smith, and Mr G. O. Rathbone. They bore the burden of office year after year, for more than ten years.

Throughout all this period Mr W. E. Copp, the former actuary of the Coventry Trustee Savings Bank, gave his services cheerfully and unstintingly as treasurer of the Cathedral Council, whose finance committee was responsible for the finances of the congregation.

It had for many years been a tradition of the Cathedral to be foremost in the diocese for its support of the Church Overseas. With a small congregation it was impossible to maintain this standard in terms of missionary offerings. Nevertheless it happily turned out that our eldest daughter, who had been a member of the congregation since childhood, was now to sail as a Church Mission Society missionary to Kenya. The congregation undertook to contribute a hundred pounds a year, to her support, which would make her "Our Own Missionary" for the Cathedral. At the same time they maintained their contributions to the other missionary societies. For a congregation to have a missionary of its own, an actual member of the congregation, forges a strong link between the Church at Home and Overseas, and stimulates as nothing else can do the willingness of people both to pray and to give.

Gradually the congregation was welded together into an intimate fellowship. A prayer-roll was issued at regular intervals with the name, address, and occupation of every regular member of the congregation (even babies) against one day of the month, and a request for prayer for that person on that day of the month; and this was widely used.

The congregation had no public meeting place outside the West Crypt. Their meeting rooms, called Palace Yard, had been totally destroyed in the war. Fortunately the Provost's house is large, and its three reception rooms and garden were always at the disposal of the congregation for every kind of committee meeting and social gathering. As a result the congregation was thrown together in an intimacy that is not ordinarily possible. The conditions created by the war were unique; they required a unique solution, and brought a unique benefit. Many of the congregation were men or women in some kind of public work— doctors, teachers, lecturers, social workers, etc. Many of them were members of committees or councils for the promotion of good causes in the civic, social, or religious life of the city and diocese. We had a few important religious groups of our own—a Mothers' Union, a Church of England Men's Society, a Prayer Group for the Healing of the Sick, each of which in its own way trained its members to take a full part in the life of the community. By such means the congregation grew to be in some measure a fellowship of the Holy Spirit.

Twelve years passed. As the new Cathedral began to rise Higher and higher on its site outside the West Crypt, it was obvious that the day was approaching when the intimacy of the small Crypt must give place to the wider fellowship of the great Cathedral. Our little congregation now began to feel that their future vocation was to be the nucleus of the much greater Cathedral congregation that was to come.

PART II. 1958 -1962

CHAPTER FIFTEEN

—

The Cathedral in the Chapel of the Cross

ON August 15th, 1958, I resigned from being Provost of Coventry after a period of twenty-five years. Six weeks later, on September 27th, the Very Rev. H. C. N. Williams was instituted as the new Provost. He came from being the rector of St Mary's Church, Southampton, a large industrial parish having close ties with the city. The church had been destroyed only a few weeks after our Cathedral, and was rebuilt and opened in Provost Williams' time. What better preparation could he have had for the great task that lay before him in Coventry of carrying the new Cathedral forward to the day of its Consecration four years ahead?

In the providence of God he and I found ourselves immediately united in a close bond of friendship and spiritual rapport. It quickly became apparent how smoothly the last stage of the growth of the new Cathedral would develop out of all that had gone before.

The Provost first gathered round him a competent staff of Cathedral clergy to work with him as a team. Canon Edward H. Patey, appointed by the Bishop as a Residentiary Canon, had been the Secretary of the Youth Department of the British Council of Churches. Canon Joseph W. Poole, appointed by the Provost as Precentor of the Cathedral and by the Bishop as an Honorary Canon, had been a Minor Canon and Precentor of Canterbury Cathedral and vicar of a large parish in the diocese of Southwark. The Rev. Simon W. Phipps, appointed by the Bishop as his Industrial Chaplain and by the Provost as Chaplain of the Cathedral, had been Chaplain of Trinity College, Cambridge.

The Rev. John D. C. Alleyne, appointed by the Provost as Chaplain of the Cathedral, had been the curate of the Provost in Southampton, and was now to assist him in the care of the Cathedral congregation. The Rev. Stephen E. Verney, the new vicar of Leamington Hastings, was appointed by the Bishop as Diocesan Missioner and by the Provost as Chaplain of the Cathedral; he had formerly been the vicar of a church in a large housing estate near Nottingham, where he had led an experiment in new church building on the "do-it-yourself" method.

Thus the personnel of the Clergy Staff of the Cathedral was qualified to go forward with the Provost to break new ground in many directions.

The first insight of the new Provost was to be convinced that the time had now come for the worship of the Cathedral congregation to be transferred from the confined spaces of the Crypt Chapels under the ruins to the larger area of the undercroft beneath the new Cathedral. Accordingly at the Provost's request Mr Basil Spence designed and prepared the whole length of the undercroft on the south side as a temporary chapel. Within the severe limitation of the curious shape of the undercroft Mr Spence achieved a remarkable success. The altar is a great slab of Columbian pine resting on two pillars of new Cathedral stone. The cross hanging behind it is made of shining metal and glass in a form which symbolizes the glory of the Charred Cross in the ruins. An open space in front of the sanctuary gives room for ceremonial movement. There is provision for more than four hundred people to sit, though in a very elongated "nave". (Figure 22.)

In the last months of his life the aged and greatly respected antiquarian, Mr John Shelton, suggested as the title for this chapel "The Chapel of the Cross". This was universally accepted as being exactly right.

Figure 22 The sanctuary and choir of the Chapel of the Cross in the undercroft of the new Cathedral. 1959.

On New Year's Eve, December 31st, 1958, the Cathedral congregation, augmented by many representatives from the diocese and city, gathered in this new Chapel of the Cross for its dedication by the Bishop. As an important element in the service there occurred the significant ceremony of "The Handing on of the Torch". For the first lighting of the altar candles after the dedication of the Chapel of the Cross I started in a procession from the back of the chapel with a torch lit from candles lighted at the last Eucharist of the year in the Crypt Chapel, where the Holy Communion had been celebrated during the whole period since the destruction. Accompanied by a small group of attendants I proceeded to the sanctuary rails, there to hand over the torch to the new Provost, who, receiving it from me, lit the altar candles for the first time on the site of the new Cathedral.

It can well be imagined with what intense joy and interest this ceremony was witnessed, not only by those who had worshipped long ago in the old Cathedral, nor only by those who had carried on the worship in the Crypt Chapel through the bleak years of ruin, but also by all those who were entering on the new and last period before the Cathedral was completed.

Here in this new chapel the Cathedral congregation settled down to their new surroundings. Under the leadership of the Provost and his staff the numbers quickly increased, until it became normal to see the chapel well filled for Sunday services. The peculiar intimacy of the services in the small crypts gave place to the inspiration of greater congregations. The sense of Christian fellowship gradually spread from the small nucleus to the now larger body of regular worshippers. Family Mattins remained a service at which a number of children attended with their parents. The week-day Offering of Prayer now began to be shared between the Chapel of the Cross under the new Cathedral and the chapels in the ruins.

Two large huts were built in the Cathedral churchyard opposite to the east end of Holy Trinity Church. These became the headquarters of the fellowship and operations of the Provost and his staff and also the means of fellowship for the various groups attending the Cathedral services.

Meanwhile throughout this period the Cathedral extended still further than before its outreach to the diocese, the city and the world. Early in his career the Provost declared his policy: "Before all else the Cathedral is the Mother Church of the diocese. All the parishes must feel that the Cathedral is their meeting point". Accordingly, parish priests have been welcomed as preachers and celebrants at the Cathedral. Parish parties have been welcomed and taken on conducted tours. Parish choirs have sung Evensong in the Chapel on the Cross. The Provost and Cathedral clergy have based their operations in the diocese upon the Cathedral itself, and they are familiar as preachers in almost every church of the diocese.

As a means of contact between the Cathedral and the community of the city a Tuesday Lunch Hour Service in the

Chapel of the Cross was started in April 1959 and has been running with remarkable success ever since. It provides a Christian meeting point where all the social and industrial elements of the community can meet on benevolent ground. The services, conducted and addressed alike by Anglican or Free Church Ministers and laymen, are an expression of Christian unity at a level where such co-operation is unrestricted by denominational regulations. They are an oasis of peace and a hill of vision for many in the midst of the distracting rush of daily life in the city.

The number of visitors from all over the world has steadily increased, as news of the nearing completion of the new Cathedral has reached every part of the earth. The body of honorary chaplains and stewards has been greatly enlarged and placed under the whole-time administration of a chief steward, Mr Leslie Bartlett. One of the large industrial firms of Coventry generously erected at their own cost a fine exhibition room at the back of the Cathedral ruins as a place where visitors might see models and pictures of the new Cathedral and samples of the materials being used in the construction.

The ruins continued to exercise their power over the minds of visitors. A prayer for international reconciliation was placed on a board in the sanctuary and used daily at a brief noontide act of prayer. The Charred Cross was treated with a preservative to make it immune from the weather for all time.

The Chapel of the Cross, like the temporary Chapel of Unity in the West Crypt in its time, now became the inspiring climax of the pilgrims' tours of the Cathedral.

The Creation of a New Choir

"A Cathedral Church is that church in the diocese where an offering is daily made to God of worship as beautiful as the words and music of man can make it."

For nearly twenty years there had been no cathedral choir in the accepted sense of the term, though a body of men and women had devotedly and effectively kept a tradition of excellent singing alive in the Cathedral services in the West Crypt.

By 1959 the time had clearly come when preparations must be made for the creation of a cathedral choir ready to take over at the Consecration in 1962. It takes a number of years to train a competent chorister. There are many difficult lessons to be learnt in singing, movement and behaviour. When a boy joins a choir already established, he learns his craft chiefly by imitating the boys already in the choir, who have themselves been in the choral tradition for many years. When all the choristers are new, the tradition of the choir has to be created from zero. Each boy has to be taught by the choirmaster from the beginning with no help from older choristers.

Fortunately for the Cathedral, when an approach was made to the Governors and the Headmaster of King Henry VIII School, Coventry's ancient grammar school, it was found that they welcomed the idea of establishing choral scholarships tenable at the school. Accordingly ten choral scholars were elected at Easter 1959, eight in 1960 and six in 1961, making a total of twenty-four boys to occupy the twenty-four stalls in the chancel of the new Cathedral. There are twelve stalls also for twelve men and there has been no difficulty in finding dedicated amateurs to fill them. The West Crypt under the ruins having now been released from its use as a temporary Chapel of Unity has become the song room for the newly-formed choir. After three years of training under the Precentor, Canon Poole, the choir has reached a standard where it can without fear meet the great responsibilities which will suddenly be thrust upon it at the Consecration.

In November 1961, the choir passed into the hands of the new organist and choirmaster, Mr D. F. Lepine, who took up his appointment at the age of thirty-two, and who holds the combined appointment of Organist of Coventry Cathedral and Music Adviser to the Coventry City Council, an experiment which is certainly unusual and perhaps unique.

With the commencement of worship in the choir and nave of the new Cathedral there is no further need of the long nave of the chapel in the undercroft, and this space reverts to its original purpose in the design as administrative rooms. But the wider end under the baptistry, with its altar, pendant cross and sanctuary, remains the Chapel of the Cross.

CHAPTER SIXTEEN

—

The Final Stages of Reconstruction

MR BASIL SPENCE, the architect of the new Cathedral, gradually achieved great fame during the years since his winning the competition in 1951. His creative ability was widely recognized by the choice of him as the architect of many important buildings throughout the country and beyond. He was elected President of the Royal Institute of British Architects in 1958 and held the office until 1960. In the Queen's Birthday Honours list of 1960 he was knighted and became Sir Basil Spence, to, the great pleasure and satisfaction of all his Cathedral friends.

The reconstruction, which had begun in 1954 with the clearance of the site, now in the years 1959-61 rapidly passed through its last phases towards completion. The *walls* had started to rise from the floor level in 1957 and after three years had reached roof level in the beginning of 1960. Thirty-four thousand stones had been used. The great height and strength of the walls as now seen took people by surprise. The view from the tower of the vast cavity between the walls below was an astonishment to sightseers.

Meanwhile the *roof* had been commenced over the Lady Chapel at the east end in the middle of 1959, and was gradually carried westwards for two years, being finished in the summer of 1961. It was formed of three layers; large slabs of reinforced concrete four inches thick lying on reinforced concrete beams; a layer of light thermostatic blocks also four inches thick; copper sheeting between a quarter and half an inch thick. The copper has come almost entirely from Rhodesia (figure 23).

Figure 23 1961. The nave roofed (top left); the porch built and nearly roofed (top right); the Chapel of Unity (bottom left).

Tubular *scaffolding* now covered the outside and filled the inside of the building, its total length being eighty miles.

The view of the new Cathedral from the Queen's Way in the ruins became completely obscured and, for reasons of safety, visitors were no longer allowed on the site.

Next the fourteen slender *columns* to bear the canopy were placed in position. In section each one is in the shape of a cross. The first one in its whole length of sixty-two feet was raised at the far north east on October 19, 1959, a moment of considerable excitement, and the last one nine months later before the canopy was started. They were made by the Woolaway Concrete Products Limited of Bridport in Dorset. Each column was made of pre-stressed concrete in three sections and each weighs almost nine tons. They rest on bronze shoes bolted to the floor (figure 24).

The *canopy* was begun in the summer of 1960, when all the columns were in place, and was finished in the early summer of 1961. The ribs were made of reinforced concrete, the square spaces between the ribs being formed of timber louvres whose slats were made of spruce from Canada.

Figure 24 The new Cathedral interior, ready for Consecration on May 25th, 1962.

The *plastering* of the interior walls was carried out during the summer of 1960. The area to be covered was vast indeed. Great care was taken in the composition of the plaster so that it should exactly meet all requirements. The white colour is the natural colour from the quarry and is constant throughout the whole thickness. The bold texture of the surface will contribute to the sense of the great height of the walls. Most important of all, attention has been paid to the acoustic property of the surface at all levels to suit all kinds of sound. The development of this plaster was done by Messrs. Caffereta with the Building Research Station and tested acoustically by the National Physical Laboratory.

The *floor* took a year to lay down, between November 1960 and early in 1962. It is formed of three kinds of British marble; black marble from the Kellymount quarries in County Kilkenny, which has been in use for building since the thirteenth century; Hadene cream-grey marble; light brown marble mottled with fossils from Darbydene near Matlock.

Inlaid in large letters right across the floor at the west end are the words:

To the glory of God this Cathedral burnt November 14 1940 is now rebuilt 1962.

To commemorate the generosity of the Canadian people in giving the new organ and in responding to the appeal for funds in 1953 (see page 107), a maple leaf eighteen inches wide cast in bronze with a surface relief is placed in the central aisle opposite the baptistry.

The *ten nave windows*, which had been finished by the Royal College of Art some years before, were put in by the firm of G. King & Son, Lead Glaziers, of Norwich during the first half of 1961.

The *baptistry windows* designed by John Piper and made by Patrick Reyntiens were put in during the summer of 1961.

The windows of the glass screen at the west end, designed and made by John Hutton were put in between phosphor bronze mullions during the summer and autumn of 1961.

The reconstruction was now taking a dramatic turn with never-to-be-forgotten moments of pleasure for those who experienced them. Owing to the completion of all the work at the east end of the Cathedral the scaffolding outside and inside could be gradually taken down from the Lady Chapel and the eastern bays of the nave. Apart from the floor and furnishings within and the tidying of the ground outside, the exact form and colour of the new Cathedral could now be seen for the first time with a view uninterrupted by scaffolding. The beauty and dignity of the exterior walls of the interior of the Lady Chapel, and of the canopy, and the light and colour of the windows, fulfilled and exceeded all our hopes and imaginings. We began to get a realistic impression of how beautiful and noble a building our new Cathedral was going to be when wholly finished (figure 25).

Figure 25 The completed nave of the new Cathedral, showing the baptistry window (centre) and the five nave windows. (Foreground) The architect, Sir Basil Spence. December 1961.

These moments were constantly to recur with the gradual completion of all the works that are yet to be described.

The *Chapel of Unity* with its peculiarly original and lively design as a crusader's tent was built during 1960 and faced during 1961 with green Westmorland slate from quarries near Coniston (see figure 23). The windows which, like the baptistry windows, are in colours only, without symbols or figures, have been designed by Margaret Traherne, trained at the Royal College of Art and at the Central School of Arts and Crafts in London.

Figure 26 1961. The nave completed; the Guild Chapel erected in concrete, ready for facing with green slate.

The circular *Guild Chapel* (figure 26) at the south east was not started until early 1961, later than any other part of the new Cathedral. Balancing the Chapel of Unity in the north west it also is faced with Westmorland stone. It has now been newly named "The Chapel of Christ the Servant", as befits the chapel of those who serve one another and the community in industry. Underneath the chapel the ground floor of the building is the chapter house for meetings of the Cathedral Chapter and other bodies. It is purposed to place in the windows the ancient glass saved from the old Cathedral.

The *Gethsemane Chapel* is the chapel at the far east end of the south aisle and was naturally completed with the nave as far as its building was concerned. The name of this chapel also has been newly conceived: "The Chapel of Christ in Gethsemane". It is the chapel of private prayer for the use especially of sufferers. It is the place where people with intense personal problems can come and "sweat great drops of blood" with Christ, sharing the comfort of "the angel of the Lord strengthening Him."

The *mural panels* were inscribed by Ralph Beyer and his assistant during the first half of 1961 after the roof was on and the stone panels had become dry. It was decided at a conference of the Provost, the Architect, the Precentor and myself that in future the best title for these mural panels would be "The Tablets of the Word".

The *porch* with its tall round columns faced with pink-grey stone and with its broad stairways was slowly built as to its deep foundations during 1960 and as to its superstructure during 1961. Two great oaken crosses, twenty-one feet by fourteen feet, have been placed high up between the pillars on the sides facing the approaches from Priory Street and from along St Michael's Avenue. They have been given by Mr Oscar Grunau of Awson Motor Carriage Company Limited, and have been made at his firm out of oak from trees about one hundred years old which grew at Tile Hill a few miles from Coventry.

Thus at the heart of our new city there is openly represented the Sacrifice of Christ—the supreme act of the redeeming love of God and the perfect example of the love of man. Whoever enters the porch will have his mind prepared by the symbol of the Crucifixion before he goes into the Cathedral to see the glories of the Resurrection and Ascension.

The *fleche*, the extremely imaginative form in modern terms of an ancient spire, is made of a lattice-work of bronze. At its top, ninety feet above the roof, is a weather-vane, designed by Geoffrey Clarke, one of the three designers of the nave windows. The *fleche* and weather-vane were separately lifted into their places by helicopters of the Royal Air Force.

The *vestries* and administrative rooms of a cathedral are an essential part of its practical equipment for worship. Fortunately in Sir Basil Spence's design ample space for these has been provided in the undercroft. As the reconstruction neared its end, and the builders retired from this area, it could be seen how best to allocate each room to its most convenient use.

Figure 27 Coventry Cathedral, old and new. (From l. to r.) The old apse and tower, the new porch, Holy Trinity Church Spire, the flèche, the new Cathedral and Guild Chapel, May 1962.

CHAPTER SEVENTEEN

—

Works of Art Completed

The Tapestry

The tapestry was begun in 1959. It has been woven in the tiny town of Felletin deep in the heart of France, not far from Aubusson, a district famous for tapestries for a thousand years. Ten of the most expert weavers, men and women, sitting side by side at the great horizontal loom, are responsible for this magnificent piece of craftsmanship. The wool used is entirely Australian, being very fine and suitable for use with synthetic dyes.

In April 1959 a small sample section of the tapestry figuring the eagle, one of the "four living creatures"; was woven and placed on exhibition in Coventry. All who saw it experienced a breathtaking wonder at the startling brightness, beauty and harmony of the colours, a presage of the glory to be revealed when finished. Its hanging in the spring of 1962 was one of the last acts of reconstruction.

The Organ

The firm of Harrison and Harrison began on the construction of the organ in January 1960. After the publication of the specifications suggestions came in from many quarters, Mr Cuthbert Harrison has been able to incorporate the best ideas from all suggestions, leaving the main conception of the specification as originally designed.

During the summer and autumn of 1961 the organ was installed in its place in the new Cathedral high up on upper and lower platforms on either side at the end of the aisles.

The Statue of St Michael and the Devil

Sir Jacob Epstein died on August 7, 1959, while his statue of St Michael and the Devil was in the later stages of its casting in bronze. This statue is therefore one of his very latest works.

Early in 1960 the work was finished. Its cost was defrayed by an anonymous donor. The statue was brought to Coventry, and erected in its place on the outside of the Cathedral. On St John Baptist's Day, June 24, it was unveiled at a ceremony which was another landmark in the story of the rebuilding of the Cathedral. One's first impression is of the great strength and compassion of St Michael. The portrayal of the Devil in the shape of modern man chained by his own limitations is equally moving.

The unveiling by Lady Epstein was preceded by a service of dedication in the Chapel of the Cross attended by a large congregation of guests invited from all over the country, clergy of the diocese, heads of industry and civic life and members of the Cathedral itself. The Bishop of Coventry in his address described the statue as deeply challenging, and said how privileged we were that at the entrance to the new Cathedral we should have the work of one of the greatest artists of this century, depicting for all time the eternal struggle for the soul of mankind between the forces of good and evil. There is little doubt that people will come from all over the world to see the statue, which may well prove to be one of the most challenging and outstanding contributions to art in our generation.

The Font

Britain's newest Cathedral is to have a font which will link it with the origin of the Christian Faith. A great rock which has stood on the hillside outside Bethlehem for thousands of years, and would have been there when Christ was born, has been brought from Bethlehem to Coventry to be the font of the new Cathedral.

Mr Frankland Dark, an architect frequently at work in the Middle East, suggested to Sir Basil Spence that this, the newest of all cathedrals, should be linked with the earliest point of the Christian religion by bringing the font—the beginning of Christian membership for all those who will be baptized in it—from Bethlehem itself.

The steps by which this huge boulder weighing three tons was chosen and then transported by land and sea from Bethlehem to Coventry have been marked by a saga of co-operation and goodwill. Much time, labour, and money were voluntarily expended by officials and businessmen of the nations involved—Britain, Jordan, Syria and Lebanon.

When the boulder finally reached Coventry, it was placed temporarily in the Queen's Way, and was unveiled by the six-year-old son of the foreman carpenter of the Cathedral reconstruction. The basin is carved out of the top of it. Simple Christian symbols are carved here and there upon it. Its final place is under the great baptistry window, raised a few inches from the floor on a small metal support.

The Inlaid Marble Floor of the Chapel Of Unity

The Chapel of Unity has always been thought of as the Chapel of the Holy Spirit, the Fountain of Love. In his original design Sir Basil Spence has proposed that the floor of the Chapel should be a mosaic symbolizing the Holy Spirit. In 1960 the people of Sweden through their ambassador and cultural attaché made it known that they wanted to give something to Coventry Cathedral. Mr Einar Forseth, the famous Swedish architect, came over to Coventry anxious to use his talents in some way for the Cathedral. It was decided that he should be commissioned to design the inlaid marble floor of the Chapel of Unity. His design was approved by the Joint Council and Reconstruction Committee. The King and

Queen of Sweden contributed towards the £5,000 raised by an appeal in Sweden to pay for the building of the floor.

Built of marble from many European countries the pattern extends from wall to wall in the Chapel of Unity. At the centre of the design is the figure of a dove, the symbol of the Holy Spirit, surrounded by the traditional emblems of the four evangelists. Circular symbols represent the five continents.

The generous gift of this magnificent floor is symbolic of the close links that bind the people and churches of Sweden and Britain together in Christian faith and in their common desire for international peace.

The Window of the Lady Chapel Entrance

The five windows of the entrance to the Lady Chapel opposite the top of the great staircase have received stained glass designed also by Mr Einar Forseth at the cost of a fund raised from the members of the Swedish colony in London by one of its oldest members, Mr Torsten Landby. English missionaries are reputed to be among the first to have taught Christianity in Sweden, and the design of the stained glass will represent them and their heroic sufferings for the Faith.

The Altars

The book of conditions for the architectural competition in 1951 began with a preface, signed by the Bishop and Provost, in which they said: "This should be the ideal of the architect—not to conceive a building and to put in an altar, but to conceive an altar and to create a building." Sir Basil Spence from the first moment of his vision of the new Cathedral has always seen the altar as the jewel-like centre of a shrine to the glory of God. As the Cathedral has clothed itself with the bright colours of the tapestry and windows, Sir Basil has conceived the idea that the altar should be prominent in contrast by its majestic simplicity and beauty.

Accordingly it is built of hammered concrete, appearing like granite, in the rough shape of an ancient oak refectory table.

It is surmounted by a thick oak board or mensa. Thus it is a true altar-table. Its massive strength and great breadth of twenty-one feet will cause it to stand out as the central object of the Cathedral. It is in shape and colour and appearance a work of art of great excellence.

Standing on the pedestal behind the altar is a large silver-gilt altar cross, designed by Geoffrey Clarke, in an abstract shape suggesting the sharpness of death, and holding at its centre an actual Cross of Nails from the ruins.

Kneelers

During the past generation many of the cathedrals and parish churches of the land have furnished themselves with colourful kneelers worked by voluntary bands of needle-women. Stimulated by their example the women of our diocese of Coventry have provided the new Cathedral with an ample supply of kneelers. The work has been organized by Lady Helen Seymour as Director, the late Miss Winifred Walker, O.B.E., as the very experienced Craft Advisor, and Mrs Walter Howard as Secretary. Sir Basil Spence produced six designs in striking modern style and colour harmony, each figuring an ecclesiastical symbol. In the great majority of the parishes of the diocese about five needlewomen have each been given a standard pattern and wools, and have laboriously worked them into the kneelers. These thousand kneelers when spread over the Cathedral will create a carpet of harmonious colours with a due reserve of variety.

The Reredos of the Gethsemane Chapel

Corresponding to the name of the chapel the reredos above the altar of the Chapel of Christ in Gethsemane depicts the whole Gethsemane scene, the disciples asleep, the Lord in agony, the Angel with the cup strengthening Him. It is designed by Steven Sykes, a lecturer at the Chelsea School of Art, who has developed a new technique of his own in the art of pictorial panel making. A black iron screen in the shape of a crown of thorns divides the chapel from the approach to it. It is designed by Sir Basil Spence and made by the Royal Engineers at Chatham.

The Woodwork

All the furniture for the sanctuary, chancel, nave and chapels has been designed by Sir Basil Spence, except the nave chairs designed by Professor R. D. Russell. The bishop's throne, provost's stall and clergy stalls have elaborate canopies.

The theme of the thorn runs through the design of all the woodwork in the chancel so that "the approach of the communicant to the altar is through an avenue of thorns."

The choir stalls are designed to be movable in order to allow the maximum flexibility of arrangement, forward to gain the close relationship needed between the two sides of the choir, backward to allow an open view from the nave to the high altar.

Many smaller works of art, too numerous to be mentioned here, have been presented as gifts to the new Cathedral by individuals and corporate bodies. They are for the adornment and equipment of the Cathedral as a place of worship of God Most High.

CHAPTER EIGHTEEN

—

The Cost and its Defrayment

WHEN the new Cathedral is quite finished and all the bills have been paid, it will be possible to state a figure for the total cost of the reconstruction. It would include the cost of the preservation of the ruins, the purchase of the land on which the new Cathedral is built, the laying of the foundations, the building of the nave and the porch, the building of the Chapel of Unity and the Guild Chapel, the provision of the great works of art, the furnishings and equipment, and all the fees and administrative expenses.

The period of reconstruction which covers the fifteen years between 1947 and 1962 has been one of almost continuous inflation, sometimes alarmingly rapid, when costs have risen out of all recognition compared to original estimates.

At the time of the writing of this history it can be stated that the total cost will be roughly £ 1,350,000.

Towards this cost the War Damage Commission is providing approximately £1,000,000 as compensation for the destruction of the old Cathedral and all its furnishings.

The balance of the cost is being provided by voluntary contributions, which may be summarized under four heads.

(i) In 1946, as has been described in Chapter seven, an appeal was launched for the new Cathedral and Chapel of Unity, which reached a total of £75,000 (net) before it had to be suddenly called off.

(ii) In 1958 with the full support of the Diocesan Conference Bishop Cuthbert Bardsley launched an appeal for £750,000 called "The Bishop's Appeal, 1958/60" as a joint appeal to raise £530,000 for the needs of the diocese and £220,000 for the new Cathedral. The appeal was launched on Ash Wednesday, 1958, with a day of continuous prayer in all churches throughout the diocese. Almost immediately visible signs of answers to these prayers could be seen in the readiness of the response of individual people within the Church. It was first and foremost from the Church that the initial response came, which was obviously right. When substantial sums had thus been raised the appeal was taken to Industry.

During the three years between the spring of 1958 and 1961 the Bishop and the organizer of the appeal, Canon E. A. Buchan, toured the diocese, meeting 120 small groups of people at little social gatherings in private houses, church halls, or hotels. It was largely from these meetings that the money was raised. When the Thanksgiving Service was held in February 1961, the total money given or promised was £590,000, of which £150,000 was for the building of the new Cathedral.

(iii) Quite apart from definite appeals, throughout the whole of the twenty-one years since the ruin of the Cathedral in 1940, there has been a continuous stream of donations, great and small, from people living in all continents of the world, who have been touched by the tragedy of the destruction or by the ideals of unity and renewal for which the reconstruction has stood.

(iv) Among the largest of individual contributions some have been remarkable enough to deserve a special mention. Lord Iliffe and his successors have given £35,000 for the reconstruction. The Canadian College of Organists gave £10,800 towards the new organ. An anonymous donor has given £27,000 for the tapestry. Another anonymous donor has given £40,000 to defray the cost of the baptistry window and the St Michael statue. President Heuss on behalf of the German Evangelical Churches has given £5,000 for the Chapel of Unity windows and Dr Adenauer on behalf of the German Government has given £4,250 for the rebuilding.

It is interesting to reflect that while the first ancient Minster Cathedral was built by the nobility, Earl Leofric and Lady Godiva, and the second by merchant princes, the Bottoners, our third and new Cathedral has been built at the cost of the nation and people.

CHAPTER NINETEEN

—

The Reconstruction Committee

By the time this story closes the Reconstruction Committee will have been at work for fifteen years. Since its members have been engaged in one of the most important national and ecclesiastical projects of this century, it is proper that their names should be recorded in the body of this book. They were appointed from time to time by the Cathedral Council and, in the case of those representing the Free Churches by the Christian Service Centre Joint Council. The original members appointed in 1947 were:

> Colonel the Hon. Cyril Siddeley, later Lord Kenilworth, chairman.
> Mr Julian Hoare, of the Coventry Evening Telegraph.
> Alderman George Briggs, J.P., former Mayor of Coventry.
> Colonel Sir Fordham Flower, of Stratford-on-Avon.
> Mr W. S. Heatley, of the Coventry Economic Building Society (representing the Free Churches).
> Mr E. J. Corbett, Manager of Barclay's Bank, Coventry.
> The Rev. D. G. Wylie, Vice-Chairman of the Christian Service Centre Joint Council, Minister of Queen's Road Baptist Church.

I, as Provost, was ex-officio member of all Cathedral committees.

The Bishop, while not a member of this committee, was invited to attend all its meetings.

Captain Norman T. Thurston was appointed secretary.

In 1949 Mr Ernest Ford, on his retirement as City Engineer of Coventry, succeeded Colonel Siddeley as chairman. In 1949 Mr Corbett retired from the committee, and died in 1951. His place was taken by Mr B. R. Masser, a well-known Coventry solicitor.

In 1954 the Rev. Gordon Wylie left Coventry; his place was taken by the Rev. R. W. Hugh Jones, Minister of Warwick Road Congregational Church. He left Coventry in 1961.

In 1955 Mr Ford died, and was succeeded as chairman by Colonel Sir Fordham Flower. Mr Masser died in the same year.

In 1956 the committee was joined by Sir Stanley Harley, Managing Director of the Coventry Gauge and Tool Company and Mr V. Oubridge, Managing Director of the British Piston Ring Company.

In 1956 Dr Bardsley succeeded Dr Gorton as Bishop, and was invited to attend all committees.

In 1958 my place as Provost was taken by the Very Rev. H. C. N. Williams; in the same year Alderman Briggs retired.

In 1959 Mr W. S. Heatley died; his place was taken by Mr W. Chinn, Director of Education of the Coventry City Corporation.

In 1959 the committee was joined by Mr G. J. T. Collier, owner of the Church Book Shop, Clerk to the Cathedral Council.

Starting their work in an office at Diocesan House the committee soon took up new quarters in 1947 in the old timbered house at 22 Bayley Lane directly opposite the south-west door of the Cathedral. Here in two small rooms on the ground floor the administration of reconstruction was carried on for the next fourteen years. The officers of the committee will never forget the tiny room where only three people had room to sit and where all-important discussions took place and epoch-making decisions were made.

The meetings of the full committee were held first in a committee room of the Council House, then through the good offices of Mr W. R. Heatley in the board room of the Coventry Economic Building Society, then in a room at Messrs

Browetts, the Cathedral solicitors, next door to the Reconstruction Offices.

In 1961 the Reconstruction Office moved to more commodious rooms in the Cathedral Office set up in the old Georgian house at 26-28 Bailey Lane, where the final stages of reconstruction and the Consecration are being planned.

Speaking as an observer of the committee, I cannot fail to place on record my admiration for its members who have cheerfully borne tremendous responsibilities, and devoted their time, wisdom and experience to the successful accomplishment of a great task. On Captain Thurston's shoulders the burden of responsibility has been heavy and incessant. His work for the new Cathedral has been done largely out of sight. In its competence, cheerfulness and devotion it has been most praiseworthy.

CHAPTER TWENTY

—

The Mission of the New Cathedral: Reconciliation

MANY times in the first part of this history I called attention to the message, which from the moment of destruction the ruins of the old Cathedral loudly declared, that, in everything which has to do with our Lord Jesus Christ, painful crucifixion will surely issue in joyful resurrection. Provost Williams from the first days of his ministry entered fully into this heritage. Standing in view of the inscription "Father forgive" on the sanctuary walls and in sight of the rising new Cathedral he became equally convinced of a further truth, namely that the purpose of the resurrection of the Cathedral is that the risen new Cathedral should become a powerful instrument in the hands of God for the reconciliation of man with God and of man with man. Reconciliation is at the heart of the Christian Gospel; it should be the chief mission of the Cathedral.

Reconciliation Between Nations

First there is in this war-scarred world a desperate need for reconciliation between people at the *international* level. Let the Cathedral preach peace in word, but also in the power of the Prince of Peace let it seek to create actual peace in the hearts and minds of the visitors to the Cathedral from the once warring nations of the world. Let it draw the people of the Churches of these nations together in Christian fellowship, and through them infiltrate thoughts and feelings of peace into the wider secular relationships of nation with nation. Let this be done on the widest possible scale, but let a sincere beginning be made at the toughest point, the long breach between Britain and Germany. Let the power of the Christian Faith operate from Coventry Cathedral as an effective means of international reconciliation.

Much has been done to give practical effect to this ideal. A Coventry Cathedral International Fellowship has been founded with a membership of those from all nations who dedicate themselves to this reconciling ministry. The old coke-house and organ chamber under the east end of the ruins has been reconditioned and decorated as an International Centre, where visitors from overseas can meet each other and also find physical refreshment. As an extension of this Centre the war-damaged vestries behind the east end of the Cathedral are being restored voluntarily by a body of young Germans called "Action for Reconciliation".

Meanwhile there has been a succession of visits of the greatest interest between the two countries. Two of these stand out as of supreme importance. In January, 1960, Bishop Otto Dibelius, the Evangelical Bishop of Berlin, visited the Cathedral, preached both on Sunday and at the Lunch Hour Service, and opened the International Centre. It was one of the great occasions in the history of the Cathedral and, indeed, the history of Coventry itself. He is a man of profound moral courage and great spiritual stature. In opening the Centre he said, "It is my prayer that this place of reunion on sacred ground may spread across Europe and fill the whole world with a new feeling of fellowship, hope and love."

In February, 1961, the Provost paid a ten-day visit to Germany, touring through Berlin, Bonn, Hamburg, Kiel, Hanover and Düsseldorf, meeting large and influential bodies of people, both religious and secular, and lecturing in each place to a great congregation on the subject of "Coventry—a symbol of reconciliation". He said: "Coventry was made a symbol of hatred and destruction. We are trying to make it a symbol of the ideal of reconciliation ..." "It is the contribution which Christianity is compelled to offer if it is not to betray its faith ... I hope for one first thing in the international ministry of Coventry Cathedral; it is that we shall establish firmly and honestly that the bond between Christians—merely because they are Christians—is sufficient to break down every other barrier."

Reconciliation between Separated Churches

No less urgent is the need for reconciliation in the *inter-denominational* field. The Church is fatally weakened in her proclamation of reconciliation while she is divided within herself. During the years since the foundation of the Christian Service Centre and Chapel of Unity in 1945 Coventry Cathedral has become increasingly known throughout the Christian world for its work for Christian unity. During the years immediately preceding the Consecration the Provost and his staff have, to a man, championed the cause of reconciliation between the Churches. Under the good Hand of God, Coventry Cathedral has become one of the centres of ecumenical importance in the world.

On September 24th, 1960, visible expression was given to the final adoption by the Cathedral of this "Mission of Christian Unity". Closely connected with the Anglican Cathedral, the walls of the new and permanent Chapel of Unity had risen from the ground to roof level, so that the Chapel could now be seen as an accomplished fact. The Joint Council felt that here was the opportunity and now was the time for the present generation to re-declare the aims of the original Declaration made in 1945. With brilliant imagination a service was composed for the laying of "The Stone of Witness" in the floor at the entrance to the Chapel, inscribed with the words "That they all may be one". Thousands of Christian people from the Christian Churches were present as worshippers and witnesses. The Bishop as chairman of the Joint Council led the congregation in great acts of penitence, worship and prayer. "We meet in the presence of Almighty

God ... to pray for the recovering of the unity of Christ's Church ... through Jesus Christ in whom we are all made one". Dr Leslie Cooke, the first Vice-Chairman of the Joint Council and a signatory of the Declaration of 1945, now a leading officer of the World Council of Churches, laid the Stone of Witness attended by a young member of the Church of England and by a young member of the Free Churches. "In the faith of Jesus Christ we set this stone to be a witness to our unity in Him. " The address was given by the Reverend R. W. Hugh Jones, the Vice-Chairman of the Joint Council. Then the Declaration was solemnly and publicly signed by the members of the Joint Council, after which the Bishop said: "... We are one in acknowledging Him (our Lord Jesus Christ) as our God and Saviour. We are divided from one another in matters of faith, order, and tradition. But Christ has made us His own, and He is not divided. In seeking Him we find one another. We have committed ourselves afresh to Him, and have covenanted with one another. We intend to stay together. We call upon churches and congregations everywhere to endorse and fulfil our covenant in their relations with one another."

Thus was the course set for the future of the new Cathedral and Chapel of Unity.

The purpose of the temporary Chapel of Unity in the West Crypt had now been fulfilled. It was therefore dismantled as a chapel and its uses transferred to the Chapel of the Cross until the completion of the new Chapel of Unity.

The whole of the financial resources of the Joint Council have been devoted to the building of the Chapel of Unity. The Christian Service Centre will therefore not be among the buildings completed at the time of the Consecration. Yet the determination to realize the ideals of united Christian service to the community as enshrined in the original proposals for a Christian Service Centre remains undiminished. It is intended that as soon as practicable a building near to the

Cathedral shall be acquired, in which all the purposes of the Centre may be fulfilled.

Reconciliation between Classes in Industry

We live in an industrial age. The diocese of Coventry is at the centre of the industrial Midlands. The vast majority of our people in town and country are involved in industry. Ever since the Industrial Revolution began, industry has tended to create bitter tensions between the various classes engaged in it, and these tensions continually lead to conflict within countries and sometimes even to war between nations.

Reconciliation between man and man and between class and class is sorely needed in the field of industrial relationships. In theory the Christian Church has a message to give and a contribution to make which is entirely relevant to this need. But a great deal of study and experiment is necessary before the Church's message and power can be brought to bear directly on the industrial situation.

Coventry Cathedral has set up what might be termed a ministry of *industrial* reconciliation under the leadership of the Industrial Chaplain with a team of part-time colleagues representing four denominations. The object of the work is to make contact with the world of industry at every level. Through contact comes a growing understanding of the problems that industry has to cope with. As this understanding grows, it becomes possible to know in what sense Christian thought and action have something to contribute to industrial affairs. The aim is to draw lay people in industry into this Christian concern for its life, so that the Church may become alive and effective at its very heart.

This can only develop over a long period of time, but it is the general experience that all levels in factory life welcome this work. Once friendship and confidence is established an enormous area of mutual concern is seen to exist.

While the work is mainly done "in the field" through friendships, discussion groups and week-end conferences, the Chapel of Christ the Servant is its focus. This circular chapel with its central altar will have cut in its floor the words: "If I, the Lord and the Master, have washed your feet, ye also ought to wash one another's feet"—a good text for industrial relations.

Reconciliation of Man With God

The starting point of all reconciliation of man with man is the reconciliation of *individual* man himself with God Himself For man in politics, man in industry, man in church can only behave towards his fellow man with the depth and intensity of love required for practical reconciliation if he is set on fire with the Love of God kindled in his heart by his own reconciliation with God. The new Cathedral is therefore committed to evangelism. Here immediately it strikes up against the most acute problem of present day Christianity, the difficulty of making the Christian Faith understandable by modern man, who has drifted so far from institutional religion with its traditional modes of expression.

Hence the Cathedral conceives its Mission to be one of using to the full all the modern techniques of communication which secular agencies have perfected—television, broadcasting, drama and the arts, study in the places where people work. Not least among these is drama. Accordingly a Coventry Cathedral Drama Council was established in the autumn of 1960 with representatives from the professional and amateur theatre, the Religious Drama Society and the world of education. In 1961 Mr Martyn Colburn was appointed as Drama Director of Coventry Cathedral, in order to lead and direct the work of this new Drama Council. He was trained as an actor at the Royal Academy of Dramatic Art and has toured the country performing and producing both mediaeval and contemporary styles of religious drama. The plan is to produce plays regularly in the new Cathedral performed by amateur groups professionally trained "as an opportunity for the awakening of Man to the glory of God". These plays will not mainly be religious in the strict sense of presenting religious scenes in dramatic form, but will be plays of first class dramatic quality in their own right, presenting with the subtle power of drama the problems of life always with the insights of the Christian Faith as the foundation of their solution.

CHAPTER TWENTY-ONE

—

Preparations for the Consecration

As the building of the Cathedral went steadily on during the late 1950s it became clear that the summer of 1962 could be definitely fixed as the time for the Consecration. It needed little imagination to realize that this would be a moment of epoch-making importance in the history not only of Coventry and the diocese but also of the nation, and the whole world. Inspired in the first place by laymen in one case and by clergy in the other, two movements came spontaneously into being with the purpose of making the Consecration period worthy of so great an occasion.

The Festival of Coventry Cathedral

At the end of 1956 two business men brought to the Bishop an idea which throughout the following years has developed into a scheme of tremendous magnitude. It is that—as the Bishop was later to put it—the whole diocese should be *en fête* to mark the Consecration with joy and thanksgiving.

The fact is that the Christian Faith concerns every living person at every point of his daily life, in home, industry and recreation. The Cathedral is the visible expression of the Christian Faith and the headquarters of Christianity in active relationship with the total community. Then the Consecration must be a matter of importance not only to Church people in their services but to all people everywhere in their common interests and activities. Hence a "Festival of Coventry Cathedral" has been organized in order that "the impact of the Consecration should reach every section of the people and every furthest place in the diocese, so that all should have an opportunity of making their contribution". Twenty-four committees have been set up to organize in city, town and village throughout the diocese activities in the fields of music, art, drama and sport, such as will not only express the joy of the people in their possession of a new Cathedral Church, but also hallow these fields of human life by association with the Christian Faith at so sacred a moment.

The Festival will last for twenty-four days. Sir Stanley Harley, Managing Director of the Coventry Gauge and Tool Company, has been the chairman of the executive committee and the Rev. C. E. Ross the organizing secretary. Their experience has been that "the whole idea of the festival has been enthusiastically received and an enormous amount of help has been received from a large circle of people in industry, trade, commerce, trade unions, authorities of the City of Coventry and of the boroughs in the diocese".

The Consecration of the People

Meanwhile it has fallen to the Provost to provide, following upon the Consecration service of the building itself, an all-embracing series of Consecration services for all sections of the Christian Church and of the community. "An attempt is being made during this festival to represent every aspect of life in the community, corporately and individually, in a comprehensive act of dedication to the vision of a community centred in obedience to God. In the programme therefore, agriculture, local government, the whole field of education, youth work, men, mothers, doctors and nurses, church workers, artists and musicians, the Armed Forces, the aged, industry and commerce, will be holding great services to represent each of their own particular activities which collectively are representative of the whole community."

But the idea of Consecration goes deeper even than this. There is a question that must be asked that is prior even to anything that will happen at the Consecration or its Festival.

Fermenting in the minds of certain groups of clergy during the years 1959 and 1960 was this thought: "The Consecration will be a great spiritual opportunity, the sort of chance which only comes to a diocese once in a thousand years. Does God really want, not merely the consecration of a Cathedral, but the consecration of a people? As the Cathedral will be given to God, so that He may dwell in it and pour His love through it, so must the people be given to God to become 'the temple of the Holy Spirit'."

The Bishop called all the clergy of the diocese together to discuss how to bring the laity into this preparation for Consecration. During the winter of 1960-61 the laity in the deaneries met with their clergy in groups of twelve to face in frank but fruitful discussion all that would be involved in such a re-consecration of themselves to the service of God in their parishes. The winter of 1961-62 saw the continuation of such discussions, but within the intimate circle of the parish congregation and its own priest.

Almost at the very time that this history of the Cathedral reaches its climax and the moment of its publication, there will take place the final acts of the Consecration of the People in preparation for the Consecration of the Cathedral. The Bishop, with himself as the chief missioner and the diocesan missioner as his assistant, is holding a great evangelistic mission in All Saints' Church, Leamington, one of the largest parish churches of the diocese, with the purpose of calling back to God all those people in the diocese who have lapsed from the Christian Faith.

The whole people of the diocese are called to forty days and forty nights of prayer from Palm Sunday to Consecration Day. During these days the Cross of Nails from the Cathedral is carried round every parish, and each parish becomes for a few hours a link in the chain of prayer.

The clergy are invited to affirm their ordination vows, and all the members of the Church are invited to affirm their baptismal promises, so that as we celebrate the cross and resurrection of Our Lord, our consecration may be taken up into His, and we may dare to pray with Him those words of compassion for all the world and of utter obedience to God which He prayed on the night of His crucifixion: "For their sakes I consecrate myself."

CHAPTER TWENTY-TWO

—

Into the Future

THE Risen Christ has been at work in His Church through the long centuries of the distant past; He has been evidently with us through the twenty years of the period now finished; He will be powerfully active through every phase of the coming years.

The chief proof of the existence and activity of the Risen Christ is His power to transform crucifixion into resurrection. This has happened in the experience of this Cathedral Church over the years since the destruction. This book has sought to tell the story of this experience.

But history repeats itself. There will again be moments and Periods of crucifixion. It cannot be otherwise in an institution which is the Body of Christ. Please God, the Cathedral will never be destroyed again. But there are sure to be times of stress and strain, of suffering and sacrifice. There is a leaven of crucifixion working in all true Christian life. But it will always issue in resurrection, again and again until the end of time. On each occasion a new evidence of the Risen Christ in the midst will be provided.

To the Provost and Chapter and Clergy and to the congregation of Coventry Cathedral in the fresh period now begun, and in every succeeding generation, may it be given to be made partakers of Christ's sufferings and to know with exceeding joy the power of His resurrection.

OTHER FIGURES

Figure 28 (l. to r.): The Rt. Rev. Mervyn C. Haigh, D.D., Bishop of Coventry 1931-42. The Rt. Rev. Neville C. Gorton, D.D., Bishop of Coventry, 1943-55. The Rt. Rev. Cuthbert K. N. Bardsley, D.D., Bishop of Coventry, from 1956.

Figure 29 (l. to r): The Very Rev. R. T. Howard, M.A., Provost of Coventry, 1933-58. The Very Rev. H. C. N. Williams, B.A., Provost of Coventry, from 1958. Lord Kenilworth, C.B.E., Chairman of the Reconstruction Committee, 1947-49.

Figure 30 (1. to r.): Ernest F. Ford, Esq., O.B.E., Chairman of the
Reconstruction Committee (RecCon), 1949-55. Col. Sir Fordham
Flower, O.B.E., Chairman of the RecCon, from 1955. Capt. N. T.
Thurston, O.B.E., Secretary of the RecCon, from 1947

Figure 31 (l. to r.): Sir Basil Spence, R.A., P.P.R.I.B.A., Architect of the
new Cathedral. Graham Sutherland, Esq., O.M., Designer of the
tapestry. Sir Jacob Epstein, K.B.E., Sculptor of "St. Michael and the
Devil"

Figure 32 (l. to r.): The Rev. L. E. Cooke, B.D., Vice-Chairman of the Joint Council, 1945-48. The Rev. D. Gordon Wylie, B.D., Vice-Chairman of the Joint Council, 1948-54. The Rev. R. W. Hugh Jones, B.A., Vice-Chairman of the Joint Council, 1955-61.

Figure 33 (l. to r.): Sir John Laing, C.B.E., Chairman of John Laing & Son, Ltd., General Contractors. T.J. Hocking, Esq., M.B.E., Superintendent Clerk of Works. A. Stocks, Esq., Contractors' Site Agent.

Figure 34 The visit of Prince Philip the Duke of Edinburgh, on July
15th 1960. With him is the Provost, the Very Rev. H. C. N. Williams.

Printed in Great Britain
by Amazon

64502332R00106